ARISE TO THE BATTLE

A Call to Arms

Dennis O'Daniel

PASTOR DOUG,

I PRAY THAT YOU BE
ENCOURAGED AND STRENGTHENED
FOR THE BATTLE. I APPRECIATE
YOUR HEART FOR THE KING!

BE BLESSED,

Dennis O. Danh

Ps. 144:1

ENDORSEMENTS

"I have known Dennis for nearly forty years. I have seen his intense study of God's Word and his strong prayer life. Everything he wrote about in this book he learned on the battlefield. His book gives us a simple but profound blueprint for spiritual warfare. Every Christian should read this book!"
– Mike Anderson / Director of Rescue Missions Outreach

"Here is a book that every new believer should read within their first few weeks of Salvation. Many battles are lost because we are not equipped with the necessary equipment that is needed for the type of war we are marching in to. This would be a great text book that is full of the Word of God for a New Believers class."
– Dr. Buddy Bell / Buddy Bell Ministries

"What an incredible job Dennis O'Daniel has done in explaining things we already knew but probably had not pondered why. Warfare is a vital part of any believer's walk whether they are seasoned or a new Christ follower. This book is eye training for warfare. It will keep your eyes focused on what's needed in the most simple way. Thank you, Brother Dennis for allowing the Lord to use you as a ready-writer in Kingdom Principles. I can assure you that at one point or another, this book will provide clear biblical and now examples to guide you into your God ordained destiny. I am confident that he will help readers move on and discover the joy of being a winner in Christ."

– Marc Jones / Pastor of Abundant Harvest Church

"Arise to the Battle is a powerful tool and an end-time army field manual for every soldier in the army of the Lord. This book opens the spiritual eyes to reveal more of God's perfect plan for His people. Not only does Dennis O'Daniel break down and explain what has been gifted to us as God's children, but he uses the book to reveal the authority that every believer should learn to walk in."

– Susan Knauff / Author,
Minister and Director of True Blessings Ministries

"Dennis, in his book "Arise to the Battle" has managed to enter upon a subject that many have misconstrued or made light of its real importance to the body of Christ. Spiritual warfare is not a new term within the church today; but having an accurate perspective to what it truly means scripturally has been somewhat misplaced in the daily affairs of men. Fortunately, Dennis has masterfully brought this back into focus and without all of the animated and far reaching imaginations that have sadly evolved into exaggerations beyond what the Bible really teaches on the subject of authority. This is a book that all should read."

– Pastor Tommy Morgan / Author and Pastor
Potter's Wheel Ministries

"This book truly is a must read for all believers. We are at war! It is important for the saints to know how to walk in victory over the enemy. This book prepares the Body of Christ for battle by revealing the heavenly arsenal available in the Kingdom of God!"

–Tim Osborn / Shout to the World Ministries

"In the hundreds of books that I have read through the years I have never come across one like the author Dennis O'Daniel has written. There are many books in the market today that promises you all sorts of spiritual warfare information that is rare of true value. This book needs to be read by every church person and every minister of the Gospel. This is great sermon materials for pastors and evangelists. The meat of the Word comes forth as Dennis gives analogies of battles from the Civil War to the spiritual onslaught of the enemy. Dennis will keep your interest as he shares from his heart what the Holy Spirit has showed and taught him. I highly recommend this book to the Body of Jesus Christ."

– Dr. Daniel Sue / Pastor of Living Word Church

DEDICATIONS

I dedicate this book to my wife, Vicki O'Daniel, who has helped me to pursue my dream and to fulfill the call of ministry on my life. Your love and sacrifice is such strength to me. I love you.

To my precious children Jennifer, Cody and Derek. My life would not have been complete without you. I love you and I am truly blessed to have the honor of being your Dad. I leave this as part of your legacy.

To these mentors: Rev. C. B. & Lorell Anderson, Rev. Kirby Hunter, Rev. Tom Starcke, Rev. Nolan Logan, Bishop Ruby E. Kile. To you I dedicate this book because of all of the wisdom and knowledge that you took the time to pour into my life. You recognized the calling on my life, your patience and love towards me I will never forget. I'll forever be in your debt. You created within me the desire to be a student of the Word of God and to plumb its depths. I hope in some way this book will help you to see that your efforts were not in vain.

ACKNOWLEDGEMENTS

I would be remiss to mention that this volume you hold in your hand would not be possible without the help of my dear friend and fellow minister Susan Knauff. Susan is the author of the book From Terror to Glory and she and her husband Mark have a wonderful ministry. Susan, without your help, patience, guidance, labor and skills, this dream would not have happened. I am forever indebted and thankful to you and Mark! God Bless you and your ministry.

To my friends, family and ministry and prayer partners; you too have helped a dream come to pass; thank you!

FOREWORD

Spiritual warfare is a term with which many are familiar, but may fall short of understanding its meaning. Even those who actively seek to engage in living a fully awake and submissive Christian life may fail to take this warfare seriously. It is also embarrassing to admit that some of us who live our entire lives dedicated to living and ministering in the power of the Spirit can go through periods of our lives in which we try all sorts of human solutions before we awaken to the thought, "Hey, this is not natural- we are in spiritual warfare here!"

Some have a theology of pre-determinism which makes the whole idea of 'spiritual warfare' seem redundant, after all, everything is so 'predestined' and under the total control of divine providence that taking seriously the concept of confronting principalities and powers and wrestling through unto victory seems ludicrous. The only problem with being ignorant of real spiritual warfare is Paul commands us not to be! (Ephesians 2)

The problem with attributing everything that happens to divine providence as if God was micromanaging the universe and doing a strange mixed job of it is that the Bible disavows such a concept throughout its pages. Why else would we be commanded to pray for the Kingdom to come on earth as it already is in Heaven so the will of God can be done here as there? The only problem with refusing to wrestle these issues is that Scripture tells us we DO wrestle! (Ephesians 6)

We are not espousing some sort of dualism in which evil and good are in an equal and opposite eternal tug of war, nor are we suggesting that God is ever at the mercy of Satan's devices, wondering how to counter them, but we are in just such a dilemma and the Holy Spirit is given to us to teach us how to deal with them one by one, if we are willing to listen and obey. Scripture repeatedly warns us that we are to be sober, vigilant, circumspect, discerning, reproving works of darkness, resisting idols, and confronting and overthrowing lies of the enemy. So it is best that we learn all we can about how to engage in this battle.

Dennis O'Daniel is uniquely qualified to address this subject, not only from Scripture, but from his own long and often perilous life experience. He offers clear straight forward Scriptural answers plus his own personal testimony of walking practically through some truly death dealing and dangerous battles in his life. It is an honor and blessing for me to be able to recommend the work and the ministry of Dennis O'Daniel to you."

– Clay McLean / Clay McLean Ministries

TABLE OF CONTENTS

PROLOGUE

Pulling into the driveway of the church Pastor Ray was feeling the heaviness surrounding him. He parked the car and as he began walking into his office, his mind already racing as he thought of the needs of the people of his congregation.

There was Peggy, a single mother of two, struggling to take care of her children.

Ricky, a young man in the congregation was battling addiction. Marsha was like a mother to so many in the church and she was now fighting disease in her body. Many in the church had financial problems. The church staff members were starting to become discouraged. The building certainly had its own needs he thought as he poured a cup of coffee and sat down at his desk. There were just so many needs and so many problems. 'Lord, I need to hear Your voice. I need Your direction,' he thought as he glanced out the window.

Feeling the weight of these thoughts pressing in on him, he knew there was only one thing to do. He dropped to his knees beside his desk and went into battle!

Chapter One

The War

There is one unmistakable certainty you must come to understand! You, my friend, are in a war! This very moment there is warfare surrounding you. There is a conflict raging around you with an intensity that far surpasses any conflict that has been fought on this earth. The stakes of this war are high and no one living is exempt from it. There is no escaping it. There is no cease-fire and no furloughs. There is certainly no ignoring it! This war is building in intensity by the seconds. Will you be a victim of this war or a victor over your unseen foe? Your decisions and actions during this war will not only affect your life but the lives of those whom you love and cherish.

The enemy that you face is unlike anything you can compare him to. Even Adolf Hitler can not compare to this enemy. If you took every evil dictator and mass murderer and combined them into one person, it still wouldn't even come close to this despot. With a fierceness, and hatred for you that is unfathomable, your very existence to him is something that he detests with a vengeance. This enemy is looking for every opportunity to attack you, oppress you and ultimately destroy you. He doesn't care if you are rich or poor. The color of your skin is of no significance. Whether you are young or old, he wants you destroyed! To think that if you ignore him that you will be exempt from his plans, or to keep him out of sight and therefore out of mind, is a mistake that will leave you vulnerable and exposed to his plans. He has hated you from birth and only one thing will ever satisfy his sickening taste for war and that is your enslavement or death.

Who is this cruel enemy? Who is it that seeks your destruction? It is the prince of darkness, the ruler of this world system and the god of this earth? Satan (Lucifer) is his name and let there be no mistake, he is active and determined to destroy mankind.

In the beginning this war actually started in heaven. Lucifer was an anointed angel but this was no ordinary angel. He walked in a special place. He was anointed, beautiful, had wisdom, walked on the Holy mountain of God. He was privileged until there was iniquity found in him, which had as its root, pride. He began to see himself above his Creator. He began to exalt himself in his own eyes and began a revolt. (Ezekiel 28: 11-19 / Isaiah 14: 12-16)

Lucifer began this revolt to arise to power. He had plans to become like God and was even able to involve others in his overthrow schemes. In scripture we find that one third of the angels followed after him. (Rev. 12: 4) Jesus testified to this conflict in Luke Chapter 10. "He said unto them, I beheld Satan as lightening fall from heaven." Jesus saw this conflict. He was a witness to it. Lucifer was cast out of heaven along with the angels who became ignorant and bought into this rebellion.

Do we not see this same root at many of the problems we face today? Men have decided that they will be their own masters. They have declared for years, "I will build my own empire," or "I will build my own kingdom!" "I" is the self-promotion that is so deadly. Pride always leads to rebellion and we can see this in so many people today. They believe that they are more than their Creator. They scoff at the idea of God and they ridicule any need of Him. (Romans 1: 21-32) By their actions they declare, "I am my own God." Sadly they have bought into the lies of the enemy and though they proudly throw out their chest with pride, they have no understanding that they are slaves in this war. Their prideful taunts that they are "free" are nothing but empty words spoken into the wind that are void of any real meaning.

The Shifting of the Battleground

God at some point began to speak forth that which He desired. He began to call forth and create His vision and the grand design of it. Light and darkness came forth at His spoken word and planets and stars were created. The magnificence of His creation was staggering. The beauty and wonder no words can adequately relate. Even as great as this was, the creation of man became His crowning creation. Man was made in His very own image. (Genesis 1:26-30, Genesis 2:8-25)

Contained within the scripture notations above, are specific keywords that give us a greater understanding of what God had planned and had envisioned for this creation called man. Those words are image, likeness, dominion and subdue. These words are power-filled words that expound on the purpose and intent of God's heart for man. They help us to understand God's declaration over man's life and purpose.

"And God said, "Let us make man in our image, after our likeness: and let them have dominion over the fish of the sea, and over the fowl of the air, and over the cattle, and over all the earth, and over every creeping thing that creepeth upon the earth." So God created man in his *own* image, in the image of God created he him; male and female created he them. And God blessed them, and God said unto them, "Be fruitful, and multiply, and replenish the earth, and subdue it:

and have dominion over the fish of the sea, and over the fowl of the air, and over every living thing that moveth upon the earth." (Genesis 1:26-28)

When we break these words down and study their Hebrew meaning, we see that they are not words without power. The word "image" means "figure or resemblance." Likeness means resemblance, concrete model, shape, similitude. "Dominion" means "to tread down, subjugate, reign or rule over and subdue means to conquer, keep under, to bring under subjection."

Do you see the significance of these words? God said I will make man in my likeness and then I will give to him the authority to rule over this creation and he shall reign over it. He was placing His creation under man's control. What an awesome thought that is! God created this man with His Spirit within him and gave him wisdom. Man was in total fellowship with God and there were no restraints in their fellowship. God came down and walked and talked with this man and not only that but God had turned over this creation to him to control.

This was something the psalmist questioned in Psalms 8:1-9.

"O LORD our Lord, how excellent is thy name in all the earth! Who hast set thy glory above the heavens. Out of the mouth of babes and sucklings hast thou ordained strength because of thine enemies, that thou mightest still the enemy and the avenger. When I consider thy heavens, the work of thy fingers, the moon and the stars, which thou hast ordained; what is man, that thou art mindful of him and the son of man, that thou visitest him? For thou hast made him a little lower than the angels, and hast crowned him with glory and honour. Thou madest him to have dominion over the works of thy hands; thou hast put all things under his feet: All sheep and oxen, yea, and the beasts of the field; the fowl of the air, and the fish of the sea, and whatsoever passeth through the paths of the seas. O LORD our Lord, how excellent is thy name in all the earth!"

In that scripture it says God made man "… a little lower than the angels." The Hebrew word for "angels" in this scripture is "Elohim" which is also the same Hebrew word meaning "God". The translators were seemingly almost hesitant to translate "angels" into the true meaning "God". They therefore made it appear that God made man "…a little lower than the angels" instead of the true meaning that man was created "…a little lower than God." Man was not created as a lower species to angels. God created man in His own likeness. God didn't make angels in his likeness; only man.

God made man with a purpose and design to be like Him. He essentially turned over the control of this His creation to His man, Adam. Then one day it all changed! A wrong decision changed it all!

We must remember the power of our decisions, for they not only affect us but everyone around us. Today it is difficult to fathom this original position that man held because we have always had to deal with this cursed earth and have always lived in the dominion after the fall. (Genesis 3:1-24)

What exactly took place during the fall? The Bible tells us that Satan was subtle, crafty and cunning. This is the way that he operates. He doesn't come to us declaring who he is or his intentions. He specifically knows how to lay a trap.

The serpent approaches Eve and begins to speak with her. He asks Eve, "Hath God said?" He was first able to get her to question what God had said. This is always his first mode of attack; to get us to question what God has declared. Eve adds to what God said and he pounces with two comebacks insinuating to her that surely she won't die and then adding that her eyes shall be opened and she will become like God. He convinces her that she will then know everything like God does.

"Now the serpent was more subtle than any beast of the field which the LORD God had made. And he said unto the woman, Yea, hath God said, Ye shall not eat of every tree of the garden? And the woman said unto the serpent, We may eat of the fruit of the trees of the garden: but of the fruit of the tree which *is* in the midst of the garden, God hath made said, Ye shall not eat of it, neither shall ye touch it, lest ye die. And the serpent said unto the woman, Ye shall not surely die: For God doth know that in the day ye eat thereof, then your eyes shall be opened, and ye shall be as gods, knowing good and evil." (Genesis 3:1-5)

The lure here was for the serpent to entice Eve into his rebellion. Remember, the serpent said, "I shall be like the most High God" and he used the same concept to entice Eve. Adam and Eve were already created in His image. They had God's nature, wisdom, and Spirit. Eve already had in a great measure the very thing that she was tempted with. Now, she looks at the fruit in a different light. It now seemed to have a new aspect to it. This is always the way the enemy operates. He seeks to make the forbidden look more appealing. He makes it glitter in a new way, yet the danger is still there. The destruction is still there. He also tells her she can handle it.

How many lives have been destroyed by believing that lie? "It won't enslave you." "You can handle that alcohol, those drugs, that pornography, that unforgiveness, hatred and bitterness." "You're strong. It won't trap you!" Does any of this sound familiar?

The definition of the word "occult" means "things that are hidden." This has been a trap of the enemy, to deceive man into searching into the realm of the spirit without the direction of God or His spirit. You must understand that God never meant for us to walk in ignorance. That is the reason for the Word. As we study and allow the Holy Spirit to guide us, we will walk in revelation knowledge. I am convinced there are some things we will not know until we are face to face with the Lord.

Now, being deceived, Eve and Adam ate of the fruit. Part of what Satan said was true, their eyes were opened. The problem was, it wasn't the way they hoped for. They saw that they were naked.

Before this they had been clothed with the Glory of God. I believe they didn't really pay much attention to their bodies before this. Now they notice and shame comes in and they seek to hide it. They sew fig leaves to cover themselves. Today mankind is still applying "fig leaves" to hide behind. He is seeking to appear to be something he is not or to try to hide his true self.

They hid themselves from His Presence. Sin and rebellion will make you want to run from the presence of God. A person immediately knows when he is wrong and the guilt of it will tend to make him turn away and hide from God because he thinks God just wants to punish him. They don't have a proper understanding of the heart of God.

Now the relationship has changed. Before, they enjoyed the fellowship and walked in the garden with God. Now faith turns to fear. Fellowship is broken and instead of embracing His presence they hide from Him. Thus man, God's crowning creation has become separated from his Creator.

God asks Adam a piercing question. One He asks people to this very day. "Adam where are you?"

Now do you think that the omniscient God did not know where Adam was? Do you think it was a game of hide and seek or that the garden was too big? No, he wasn't asking for Adam's "physical" location. God made Adam declare his "spiritual" location. God asks us today, "Where are you? What is your condition?"

Adams responded, "I was afraid." His faith was now twisted into the perversion of fear. His communion with the loving Creator was now twisted into something that was ruled by a fear of his Creator.

"I was naked." Adam was saying, "I have rebelled. I am uncovered in my fault. It is open before you and I see my nakedness before you. I see the distance between us. I deny though my guilt. It was the woman's fault and you gave her to me."

Don't we see that played out today? Our sin is always someone else's fault or somehow man figures a way to put the blame on God. Suddenly his relationship with Eve changes. She is the problem. If only God would change my husband, wife, children, relatives, friends, etc. Yet, maybe the problem lies within you.

Eve follows suit claiming, "It was the serpents fault." Already we see this operating and it has continued to operate to this day. Unless we own up to our responsibility, we will always shift the blame. People often hurt us and even deceive us. It is how we respond and the decisions that we make that affect our lives. You have to decide how you will react to these situations for the rest of your life.

God addresses Eve, "Who told you? What revealed this to you? Was it not your disobedience?"

God doesn't buy into the blame game. God will always get to the root of our problems. The fig leaves won't work. He deals with the core issues of our lives.

What had Adam done? He rebelled and he willingly gave in to rebellion. Notice the scripture says Adam was with Eve. He was right there with her. Adam was not away tending the garden. He wasn't away somewhere playing with the animals or lying beneath a tree. Adam was right there! Sorry men, we can not blame the women any longer. Yet Eve was deceived and Adam was not.

"And Adam was not deceived, but the woman being deceived was in the transgression." (I Timothy 2:14)

While Eve was greatly deceived, Adam was not but went willingly into agreement, knowing that it was wrong. In doing so, he gave up his authority and handed it over to this fallen angel who then began to rule this earth system. The curse with all its fury was unleashed into this earth. Man now became subject unto all the power of the curse, ruled now by satan and falling under his dominion.

It was the equivalent of treason. Adam, instead of exercising his authority and driving the serpent out, stepped aside and handed him the keys. Now God has to deal with man in a new way. First he sends man out from the garden, not to just punish him but to protect him.

"And the LORD God said, Behold, the man is become as one of us, to know good and evil: and now, lest he put forth his hand, and take also of the tree of life, and eat, and live for ever." (Genesis 3:22)

God could not allow Adam and Eve to stay in this condition, which would have happened if they had eaten of the Tree of Life and lived forever. He didn't want them permanently condemned, living forever in the fallen state that they were in. It wasn't the "physical life". Adam lived over 900 years before he died physically. It was the "fallen condition" that man was in that separated him from God. Now every man born of Adam and Eve would be born separated from God; born under the dominion of the ruler of darkness. (Romans 5:12-21)

Now Adam's relationship to this earth changed and he was not ruler and he did not have the dominion nor was he in control. He has bowed his knee to a fallen angel and made him lord over this earth.

Man became subject to the laws that govern this realm which are the laws of sin and death. This is what many people miss today. Every man born after Adam was born into slavery. We were born in bondage, born into the kingdom of darkness and separated from God. There was only one born out from under Satan's lordship.

I'm going to say something that will shock you. You are not a sinner needing redemption because of what you do. You do the things you do because of your nature. You have fruit that is sinful because of your nature. You were born separated from your Creator. You must be redeemed. Often people think that their loved one, who was a good person, and never hurt anyone, who was honest and caring and loving, obviously must have made it into heaven. However, if that loved one did not receive salvation through Jesus, there is no other way to make it into heaven. You don't achieve heaven by works. It can only come by believing in Jesus and receiving salvation by faith.

"Knowing that a man is not justified by the works of the law, but by the faith of Jesus Christ, even we have believed in Jesus Christ, that we might be justified by the faith of Christ, and not by the works of the law: for by the works of the law shall no flesh be justified." (Galatians 2:16)

We are born needing redemption. We are born needing to be delivered from this bondage that we are born into. We can only obtain redemption through Jesus. (Romans 10:3-10)

"Neither is there salvation in any other: for there is none other name under heaven given among men, whereby we must be saved." (Acts 4:8-12)

There is no other way to God. Some are deceived into believing that is a narrow minded thought. Truth is narrow and direct. It is not gray or all encompassing. This is the lie and deception of the enemy that wants your soul.

The message of the Gospel is redemption and freedom! Man has watered down the message of the Gospel. The message is not only about receiving the sacrifice of Jesus and believing on Him and making it to heaven one day. It is to redeem man back to his position in God's plan. Redemption to our rightful place, the way God meant when He created man. The Gospel is that we, through Jesus Christ, have been redeemed from enslavement and bondage and placed from one kingdom back to God's Kingdom!

"Giving thanks unto the Father, which hath made us meet to be partakers of the inheritance of the saints in light: Who hath delivered us from the power of darkness, and hath translated us into the kingdom of his dear Son: In whom we have redemption through his blood, even the forgiveness of sins: Who is the image of the invisible God, the firstborn of every creature: For by him were all things created, that are in heaven, and that are in earth, visible and invisible, whether they be thrones, or dominions, or principalities, or powers: all things were created by him, and for him: And he is before all things, and by him all things consist. And he is the head of the body, the church: who is the beginning, the firstborn from the dead; that in all things he might have the preeminence. For it pleased the Father that in him should all fulness dwell; And, having made peace through the blood of his cross, by him to reconcile all things unto himself; by him, I say, whether they be things in earth, or things in heaven. And you, that were sometime alienated and enemies in your mind by wicked works, yet now hath he reconciled in the body of his flesh through death, to present you holy and unblameable and unreproveable in his sight." (Colossians 1:12-25)

We were transferred into His kingdom when we are born again!

"[The Father] has delivered *and* drawn us to Himself out of the control *and* the dominion of darkness and has transferred us into the kingdom of the Son of His love, in Whom we have our redemption *through His blood,* [which means] the forgiveness of our sins." (Colossians 1:13-14 AMP)

"But unto every one of us is given grace according to the measure of the gift of Christ. Wherefore he saith, When he ascended up on high, he led captivity captive, and gave gifts unto men. (Now that he ascended, what is it but that he also descended first into the lower parts of the earth? He that descended is the same also that ascended up far above all heavens, that he might fill all things.)" (Ephesians 4:7-11)

This is the story of the Gospel!

The purpose of this chapter is to show you the history of this war. This is why there had to be the virgin birth of Jesus. Man lost the authority and dominion and it would take a man to get it back. It would have to be someone born out from the dominion of satan and someone who would be born free from the kingdom of darkness!

"And so it is written, the first man Adam was made a living soul; the last Adam *was made* a quickening spirit. Howbeit that *was* not first which is spiritual, but that which is natural; and afterward that which is spiritual. The first man *is* of the earth, earthy: the second man *is* the Lord from heaven. As *is* the earthy, such *are* they also that are earthy: and as *is* the heavenly, such *are* they also that are heavenly. And as we have borne the image of the earthy, we shall also bear the image of the heavenly. Now this I say, brethren, that flesh and blood cannot inherit the kingdom of God; neither doth corruption inherit incorruption." (1 Corinthians 15:45-50)

Jesus took on the form of man. He was born out from under the dominion of the ruler of this world. Jesus was born as Adam was created. He was born connected to the Father. Without the virgin birth there would not be the redemption of man.

God made His proclamation or edict of war, back in the garden.

"And the LORD God said unto the serpent, Because thou hast done this, thou *art* cursed above all cattle, and above every beast of the field; upon thy belly shalt thou go, and dust shalt thou eat all the days of thy life: And I will put enmity between thee and the woman, and between thy seed and her seed; it shall bruise thy head, and thou shalt bruise his heel. Unto the woman he said, I will greatly multiply thy sorrow and thy conception; in sorrow thou shalt bring forth children; and thy desire *shall be* to thy husband, and he shall rule over thee." (Genesis 3:14-16)

"And the Lord God said to the serpent, Because you have done this, you are cursed above all [domestic] animals and above every [wild] living thing of the field; upon your belly you shall go, and you shall eat dust [and what it contains] all the days of your life. And I will put enmity between you and the woman, and between your offspring and her Offspring; He will bruise *and* tread your head underfoot, and you will lie in wait *and* bruise His heel." (Genesis 3:14 AMP)

The definition of enmity found in the Hebrew translation means hostility and hatred. God was declaring there will be hostility, a conflict, and a war between the Seed and Satan! A war would occur between the Kingdom of God and the kingdom of darkness!

Jesus even recognized the fact that Satan was the ruler of this world:

"I will not talk with you much more, for the prince (evil genius, ruler) of the world is coming. And he has no claim on Me. [He has nothing in common with Me; there is nothing in Me that belongs to him, and he has no power over Me.]" (John 14:30 AMP)

"Now the judgment (crisis) of this world is coming on [sentence is now being passed on this world]. Now the ruler (evil genius, prince) of this world shall be cast out (expelled)." (John 12:31 AMP)

"About judgment, because the ruler (evil genius, prince) of this world [Satan] is judged *and* condemned *and* sentence already is passed upon him." (John 16:11 AMP)

Jesus said Satan was the ruler, prince of this world. We see this in the temptation in the wilderness between Jesus and Satan. (Luke 4:1-13)

Satan showed Jesus the kingdoms of this world and said, "If You worship me, I will give You the power and the glory of these kingdoms."

Jesus did not argue with him about his ability to do this. Jesus did not say, "Hey it's not yours to offer!" It would have been a hollow temptation, empty, if it weren't grounded in fact. They were under the dominion of Satan.

Jesus would one day have that dominion back and He knew it. He would purchase it legally. The day would come when He would strip Satan of the keys. The battle lines have been drawn. God has issued this proclamation of War! The focus is no longer the Throne of Heaven, but now it wages over the souls and destinies of man!

Chapter 2

He Is a God of War

It is a very important thing the way that we view God. To focus on just one aspect of Him is to hold an unbalanced view. He is a God of love, mercy, and kindness. He is our father, protector and provider. He has all of these attributes but let us not forget the others, as well. He is holy, righteous, and He is judge. He is God and reigns supreme! There is none like Him.

When reading and studying the Word of God, we can approach it from three different views.

First, the Word is God's love letter to man, revealing His thoughts and plans for man and His great care and concern for us. The Word is a revelation of His love for man and the extremes that God would go to in order to restore man to his rightful place in Him. God's purpose for man has not changed, and in the Word we find Him revealing His heart, and unfolding the vastness of His love, which at times is incomprehensible. One of the main reasons the Word was written was to reveal this to man.

"For God so loved the world that he gave his only begotten Son, that whosoever believeth in him should not perish, but have everlasting life." (John 3:16)

"Who shall separate us from the love of Christ? *Shall* tribulation, or distress, or persecution, or famine, or nakedness, or peril, or sword? As it is written, for thy sake we are killed all the day long; we are accounted as sheep for the slaughter. Nay, in all these things we are more than conquerors through him that loved us. For I am persuaded, that neither death, nor life, nor angels, nor principalities, nor powers, nor things present, nor things to come, nor height, nor depth, nor any other creature, shall be able to separate us from the love of God, which is in Christ Jesus our Lord." (Romans 8:35-39)

Second, we can consider the Word of God as a legal binding document. It is a revelation of our covenant with God. It shows God's purpose and intent and what He has bound Himself to in His covenant promises to us. When you can grasp the fact that God has bound Himself to His Word with total abandonment and He will not violate what He has decreed it becomes more alive and you see it as His promissory note to you. Not only that but God had His covenant, signed and sealed by the Blood of Jesus! It is legally binding in the spirit realm. It reveals the rights of those of us who become His redeemed, and it states what belongs to us because of the price of that redemption, which was paid in full. Covenant is one of the most powerful things on this earth. It is where two come into a union where the resources, power, provisions, strength of each belong to one another usually solemnly and attested by a sign or symbol of that union. Each will swear to harm or hurt coming to their self if they violate the agreement. God is a God of covenant.

"My covenant will I not break, nor alter the thing that is gone out of my lips." (Psalms 89:34)

"Praise ye the LORD. I will praise the LORD with *my* whole heart, in the assembly of the upright, and *in* the congregation. The works of the LORD *are* great, sought out of all them that have pleasure therein. His work *is* honourable and glorious: and his righteousness endureth for ever.

He hath made his wonderful works to be remembered: the LORD *is* gracious and full of compassion. He hath given meat unto them that fear him: he will ever be mindful of his covenant. He hath shewed his people the power of his works, that he may give them the heritage of the heathen. The works of his hands *are* verity and judgment; all his commandments *are* sure. They stand fast for ever and ever, *and are* done in truth and uprightness. He sent redemption unto his people: he hath commanded his covenant for ever: holy and reverend *is* his name." (Psalms 111:1-9)

"And said, I beseech thee, O LORD God of heaven, the great and terrible God, that keepeth covenant and mercy for them that love him and observe his commandments." (Nehemiah 1:5)

"For ever, O LORD, thy word is settled in heaven." (Psalms 119:89)

As we become settled in our hearts that God is a God of covenant it is easier for our faith to operate and become unshakeable in our trust in Him. He has said He will not break or alter it. He has bound Himself to it because of His integrity. This is such a powerful truth to understand. This makes me know that what God has declared will come to pass with a certainty and that whatever God has spoken and promised He will make happen because of covenant.

Thirdly, the Word of God can be viewed as a manual of war. The guidelines of warfare, His principles of warfare, even tactics, strategy, and code of conduct in warfare is contained in the Word of God. No army would be affective without these. We must be aware that God is a God of war and has given His edict of war. Now, in this engagement He is the Commander! We move into position as He directs while using the strategy He requires. One of the most amazing things we see in scripture is the use of military type terminology all throughout the entire book. Two kingdoms are at war; light versus darkness!

"The LORD *is* a man of war: the LORD *is* his name."
(Exodus 15:3)

"Or hath God assayed to go *and* take him a nation from
the midst of *another* nation, by temptations, by signs, and
by wonders, and by war, and by a mighty hand, and by a
stretched out arm, and by great terrors, according to all that
the LORD your God did for you in Egypt before your eyes?"
(Deuteronomy 4:34)

"When thou goest forth to war against thine enemies, and
the LORD thy God hath delivered them into thine hands, and
thou hast taken them captive." "(Deuteronomy 21:10)

"I say, *sayest thou*, (but *they are but* vain words) *I have*
counsel and strength for war: now on whom dost thou trust,
that thou rebellest against me?" (Isaiah 36:5)

"And this man went up out of his city yearly to worship and to sacrifice unto the LORD of hosts in Shiloh. And
the two sons of Eli, Hophni and Phinehas, the priests of the
LORD, *were* there." (1 Samuel 1:3)

The word "hosts" is the Hebrew word "tsebaah" which
means a mass of people, organized for war (army), a battle
company or soldiers. It is translated to host 393 times, war
41 times, army 29 times, battle 5 times. This word portrays
God as a commander over a group of people for war. He is
called the Lord of hosts 81 times in scripture.

People often talk of the land of Canaan that God gave the
children of Israel, as a "type of Heaven," however I believe
it is a "type of our overcoming life in the Lord". In leading
the people to Canaan there was war along the way. We see
this as they went throughout their time in the wilderness.
Even when they arrived at Canaan, they had to war in order
to take the land. The children of Israel had battles to walk
through in order to receive the land that had been promised.
Jericho was the first battle in the land.

Imagine the Israelites traveling for such a long time,
hearing over and over again that they are going to the land

that God had given them, the land of plenty that flowed with milk and honey, and yet when they finally arrive, they find out they have to war to even possess the land! It was everything God had promised and God had indeed given it to them, yet they had to battle to take it!

There will be no war in Heaven. Warring will be over. I believe it shows us that though God has bought our redemption and we have benefits according to our covenant promises we must contend with the giants and walled cities the enemy has planted before us in our paths. Remember, Jesus has won the victory but we enforce that victory.

This is a war to take back what the ruler of darkness has stolen. He is an outlaw and will refuse to just hand it over. This is why people fail to obtain the promises because they have a misunderstanding of warfare. They buy into the falsehood that everything will happen because of God's will. This is not true! There is a battling that sometimes is necessary to obtain the promises, as we march forward to take the land. We are trained for this.

"He teacheth my hands to war; so that a bow of steel is broken by mine arms." (2 Samuel 22:35)

"He maketh my feet like hinds' *feet*, and setteth me upon my high places. He teacheth my hands to war, so that a bow of steel is broken by mine arms. Thou hast also given me the shield of thy salvation: and thy right hand hath holden me up, and thy gentleness hath made me great. Thou hast enlarged my steps under me that my feet did not slip. I have pursued mine enemies, and overtaken them: neither did I turn again till they were consumed. I have wounded them that they were not able to rise: they are fallen under my feet. For thou hast girded me with strength unto the battle: thou hast subdued under me those that rose up against me. Thou hast also given me the necks of mine enemies; that I might destroy them that hate me. They cried, but *there was* none to save *them: even* unto the LORD, but he answered them not." (Psalms 18:33-41)

"Blessed *be* the LORD my strength, which teacheth my hands to war, *and* my fingers to fight." (Psalms 144:1)

God is a God of war and He has always led His people into warfare to fulfill His purpose and plans with all of it playing a part in this war between the kingdoms. It is without question that we must learn the art of war from Him. He has promised us victory if we follow Him and stay in covenant with Him. We must receive our instructions from Him and let Him dictate the movements of the troops, the point of assault, the strategy and tactics that He wants employed. Our marching orders come from Him, under His guidance. Many people have been defeated because they did not listen to His commands or follow His strategy. Make no mistake, this warfare is intense and to launch into it untrained and undisciplined will cost you. One of the main reasons for boot camp in the armies of today is the need for knowledge and discipline, to learn how to obey orders when given, to instill into the soldier discipline and order. The soldier needs to learn weaponry and the proper function of it. He also needs to understand and comprehend the strategy. Survival is taught! All of these things are necessary for an army to be at its best. Many people have suffered defeat because they tried to fight with their own strength and wisdom and they either became grievously injured or ended up a casualty of war. Why? It is because they failed to follow instruction and in war this mistake will cost you. God will train you for battle for He knows the strategy, the tactics, and the encampments of the enemy.

Recently I began to become very interested in the Civil War and I was compelled to read more and study more about this great conflict in our history. Although at first I couldn't understand why I was so drawn to it, I would later come to realize that the Lord wanted to use this example to show me some important key facts about warfare.

In my course of study and reading, it didn't take long for me to realize how much I did not understand about this war or the time period in which it took place. I really didn't understand the full magnitude of this conflict. I wanted to know more.

As I read there was one thing that really began to stand out in my mind. Though the Union Army had better supplies and truly outnumbered the Confederate Army, it wasn't enough for the longest time. There were several times the war could have been over if the Union Army had been better disciplined and instructed. The war could have been over within a year instead of it taking four long and bloody years. A lack of discipline and order caused the Union Army to be in disarray and even though it had far superior numbers it was ineffective. A lack of leadership in the field and in the command led to defeat after defeat for the longest time.

General Robert E. Lee was often called The Gray Fox because of his understanding of war and his cunning ability to strategize made him capable of defeating the Union Army, though he was outnumbered. In warfare it must be understood how important good leadership, knowledge, strategy, order and discipline are necessary.

We see this also in the scripture with King David and his army.

"All these men of war, that could keep rank, came with a perfect heart to Hebron, to make David king over all Israel: and all the rest also of Israel *were* of one heart to make David king." (1 Chronicles 12:38)

As we look at this army that began to gather to David we see that they were brave, they were skillful with their weapons, they were swift, and they were mighty men. One little phrase that seems to be hidden in all these descriptions is the phrase "that could keep rank". This speaks of order and discipline. It was not enough to be brave skillful men; they needed to know order as well.

Sadly, I have watched people step out, in this war, who were good people with good intentions. They wanted to defeat the enemy but ended up a casualty because they lacked knowledge, they would not submit to training, and they lacked discipline and order. They stepped into the arena of war and were not ready for the battle.

Notice that these men mentioned in I Chronicles kept rank, and they understood authority and commands. There is an important fact here and this is one area that we must grasp. To move in authority you must learn to be under authority. Even in this army of the Lord, there is the need to keep rank.

It is true that we as believers have authority in Jesus, and we have been given the right to use that authority but it will only be affective as we stay under authority. Too many people end up as casualties because they have gone out on their own not being under proper authority. They prematurely think that they know best, that they can do it better but they are ready only to suffer defeat because they acted on their own.

When we begin to realize how in scripture, military terminology is used over and over again it should bring this understanding to the forefront; we are in a war.

"*Every* purpose is established by counsel: and with good advice make war." (Proverbs 20:18)

"For by wise counsel thou shalt make thy war: and in multitude of counselors *there is* safety." (Proverbs 24:6)

The Apostle Paul often alluded to war:

"Fight the good fight of faith, lay hold on eternal life, whereunto thou art also called, and hast professed a good profession before many witnesses." (1 Timothy 6:12)

"I have fought a good fight, I have finished *my* course, I have kept the faith." (2 Timothy 4:7)

"Thou therefore endure hardness, as a good soldier of Jesus Christ. No man that warreth entangleth himself with the affairs of *this* life; that he may please him who hath chosen him to be a soldier." (2 Timothy 2:3-5)

Even Jesus spoke of it:

"Think not that I am come to send peace on earth: I came not to send peace, but a sword." (Matthew 10:34)

Jesus spoke of a division or separating that would happen. We must understand the way God looks at things, for He sees only two types of people: those in the kingdom of darkness (non-covenant) or those in the Kingdom of light (covenant). There is no gray and no in between. These who are in the Kingdom of light are to be trained and equipped for the warfare that awaits them. They become instruments of war designed by God to destroy the enemy and free the captives. These are the ones who seek to obey every command and fulfill the mission that God has instructed them to do. A warrior is a lover that is devoted to his Lord. He will love the King of Glory and fight the prince of hell.

Chapter 3

Knowing the Enemy

It is absolutely crucial that you know your enemy! This lack of understanding is too costly a price to pay. Anyone who enters a conflict or battle, who does not have a proper understanding of the strategies of their opponent, has already set themselves up for defeat or a delay in victory. One must know their opponent; their tactics and strategies, their strengths and their weaknesses and their size and armament. One major key in any war is obtaining intelligence on the enemy. Espionage and spying became a big business. Why? Intelligence: Knowledge: Insight to know and understand the opponent.

One reason people in the Body of Christ have been defeated is because they did not take the time to learn who or exactly what they were fighting.

"My people are destroyed for lack of knowledge: because thou hast rejected knowledge, I will also reject thee, that thou shalt be no priest to me: seeing thou hast forgotten the law of thy God, I will also forget thy children." (Hosea 4:6-7)

Notice in the scripture reference that God said that it was because they lacked in the area of knowledge. We are not only required to know God and His ways but to also know the enemy and his tactics as well. This is a principle we must grasp that is applicable in all areas of our lives. Any area we lack knowledge in opens an avenue of us to be taken advantage of.

I remember when I played football in school. Part of the preparation was for the team to learn our plays and then in return having some of those from our own team run the opponents plays both on the offense and defense so that we could know ahead of time and be prepared for how they ran their game. In the highly competitive sports arena information is valued. Coaches will watch game films for hours, watching the other teams to learn everything that they can while closely observing their key players, their tendencies in certain situations, who their best players are and they even look for the weaknesses in the team. Because it becomes so critical they will even look for minute things such as noticing this quarterback who always licks his fingers when he is going to pass or the running back who always leans in the direction he is going to run. It becomes this critical to know and watch for signs. Things that most would never notice are the things that the coaches and scouts look for in order to get ahead. There are teams that will not allow anyone to attend their practices and playbooks are guarded like a national treasure and information is valuable and worth any price. Knowledge is the key!

There are two extremes we can see regarding the treatment of our opponent Satan. On one hand he is portrayed as a little red suited creature with a pitchfork with a little devilish sense of humor; or said not to exist at all. On the other there is this all-powerful foe that God just barely wins out over. Both of these pictures are wrong. We have to get a balanced viewpoint. We are to know and understand how the enemy of our soul operates.

"Lest Satan should get an advantage of us: for we are not ignorant of his devices." (2 Corinthians 2:11)

Devices are defined as meaning intellect, disposition or thought. The enemy has a purpose; he has traits about him that we must learn. The enemy works on purpose and he has a strategy designed to defeat you.

"Be sober, be vigilant; because your adversary the devil, as a roaring lion, walketh about, seeking whom he may devour: Whom resist stedfast in the faith, knowing that the same afflictions are accomplished in your brethren that are in the world." (1 Peter 5:8-9)

The scriptures point out here that the enemy walks about and he is searching and looking for prey. We can see strategy, purpose, planning. He looks for the weak, wounded, and ignorant. The enemy can't devour just anyone. Notice it says that he looks for whom he may devour. He is not all-powerful and he can't devour everyone. Only those who are in a position to be devoured fall into this category. Notice, it states "like a lion" and that it did not say he is a lion. As a lion stalks his prey looking for a chance to attack, he stalks as well, looking for his next victim and looking for the best opportunity to attack. A lion will look for the weak or wounded and then tries to separate them from the rest and to isolate them. A lion will lie low in the grass in order to hide its movement. He operates with intent or purpose. In comparison, the enemy loves the darkness for this purpose as well; it hides his movements. A lion does not roar till after the kill. Neither is the enemy going to announce his presence. He counts on weakness and ignorance to cloak his coming at you.

"Put on the whole armor of God that ye may be able to stand against the wiles of the devil." (Ephesians 6:11)

The definition of wiles is to lie in wait, schemes, strategies, and methods. Yes, the devil plans and schemes against you. Are you ready to understand that the enemy of your soul has a planned attack against you? He has studied you and has a plan of attack against you and he has studied you enough to know your weaknesses and minute responses. He knows how to plan his battle. This is why knowledge of his ways is important in your battle against him. So many people have failed to grasp this and it has cost them dearly.

Our enemy is described in scripture as our adversary, Lucifer, Satan, slanderer, Apollyon, destroyer, prince of this world, angel of light, god of this world, father of lies, accuser of the brethren, evil one, serpent, thief, Beelzebub (dung god; lord of flies). These are titles given to him in the word of God. They give us insight as to who he is and how he operates. By understanding these we can begin to gain the upper hand in the battle and we can successfully wage our warfare.

Again, he is not all-powerful or all knowing but he has strategy and tactics that he uses. To accomplish this he has a variety of operations and methods. He perverts, distorts truth, deception, counterfeits, lies, fear, intimidation and these are just a few of the tools he uses to accomplish his attacks.

Believe it or not the kingdom he rules is not a haphazard or chaotic group. Just as any army is organized and has order, the kingdom of darkness also has ranks and order.

"Finally, my brethren, be strong in the Lord, and in the power of his might. Put on the whole armor of God, that ye may be able to stand against the wiles of the devil. For we wrestle not against flesh and blood, but against principalities, against powers, against the rulers of the darkness of this world, against spiritual wickedness in high *places*." (Ephesians 6:10-12)

Principalities: This word in the Greek is archas: chief rulers, leaders, highest rank

Powers: This word in the Greek is exousias: authorities, those who derive their power from chief rulers

Rulers of the Darkness: This word in the Greek is kosmokratopas – rulers, world rulers

Spiritual wickedness: This is in the Greek pneumatika ponerias – wicked spirits.

Weymouth says: "but with the despotisms, the empires, the forces that control and govern this dark world – the spirited hosts of evil arrayed against us in the heavenly warfare."

"For we are not wrestling with flesh and blood [contending only with physical opponents], but against the despotisms, against the powers, against [the master spirits who are] the world rulers of this present darkness, against the spirit forces of wickedness in the heavenly (supernatural) sphere." (Ephesians 6:12 (AMP)

So we can see that we are surrounded by wickedness and that they have an order to their movement. An example of this we find in the Old Testament book of Daniel that will illustrate this to us even better. As you read the scripture reference below, keep in mind that things happen in the spirit realm and then manifest in this earth.

"And [the angel] said to me, O Daniel, you greatly beloved man, understand the words that I speak to you and stand upright, for to you I am now sent. And while he was saying this word to me, I stood up trembling. Then he said to me, Fear not, Daniel, for from the first day that you set your mind *and* heart to understand and to humble yourself before your God, your words were heard, and I have come as a consequence of [and in response to] your words. But the prince of the kingdom of Persia withstood me for twenty-one days. Then Michael, one of the chief [of the celestial] princes, came to help me, for I remained there with the kings of Persia. Now I have come to make you understand what is to befall your people in the latter days, for the vision is for [many] days yet to come. When he had spoken to me according to these words, I turned my face toward the ground and was dumb. And behold, one in the likeness of the sons of men touched my lips. Then I opened my mouth and spoke. I said to him who stood before me, O my lord, by reason of the vision sorrows *and* pains have come upon me, and I retain no strength. For how can my lord's servant [who is so feeble] talk with this my lord? For now no strength remains in me, nor is there any breath left in me. Then there touched me again one whose appearance was like that of a man, and he strengthened me. And he said, O man greatly beloved, fear not! Peace be to you! Be strong, yes, be strong. And when he had spoken to me, I was strengthened and said, Let my lord speak, for you have strengthened me. Then he said, Do you know why I have come to you? And now I will return to fight with the [hostile] prince of Persia; and when I have gone, behold, the [hostile] prince of Greece will come. But I will tell you what is inscribed in the writing of truth *or* the Book of Truth. There is no one who holds with me *and* strengthens himself against these [hostile spirit forces] except Michael, your prince [national guardian angel]." (Daniel 10:11-21 (AMP)

Notice this angel said that it was the prince of Persia. He was not talking about a natural man but the spirit set up over Persia. Next he says the prince of Greece is coming and there is more fighting to be done. If you study history you will find the Grecians defeated the Persian Empire. It happened in the spirit realm first and then in the natural.

The enemy sets up ruling spirits (or principalities) over nations, cities, governments, states and regions. I have flown into areas and felt the atmosphere heavy with the presence of the darkness. It is real and it takes place. I believe the enemy sets up strongholds over these places with bloodshed, lust, greed, witchcraft, poverty, and spiritual darkness. There are groups that come over to this country and speak curses over the lands and waters of our great nation. They are dedicated to the destruction and defeat of this nation. So there is a strategy of the enemy and one thing can be said of him, he is certainly persistent.

Though we know that this is how the enemy operates, we have been given the way to defeat this because of what Jesus accomplished at the cross. Through our relationship with Jesus Christ, we have the authority to break these things in His precious Name and to accomplish all that God would have us to do. We walk in an area of authority that Daniel did not walk in. We never see Jesus or the apostles having to break all of this in order to minister in authority and with great signs and wonders. They walked in authority and I will share more on this topic in a later chapter. This is an area of warfare that a person must be under the direction of the Lord of Hosts to engage in. At times I believe a person will be instructed to bind these forces but only at the direction of the Lord and never should we think that the enemy or anyone else will stop what God wants accomplished.

We have seen some facts about our enemy now let us go into his arsenal, his firepower and see some of the way he operates. One of the main weapons he uses is deception. This is a powerful one!

"For such *are* false apostles, deceitful workers, transforming themselves into the apostles of Christ. And no marvel; for Satan himself is transformed into an angel of light. Therefore *it is* no great thing if his ministers also be transformed as the ministers of righteousness; whose end shall be according to their works." (2 Corinthians 11:13-15)

The word transformed means disguised or masquerading as truth when in reality it is false.

He does not come boldly declaring, "Hey I am the Devil full of lies and deceit, and what I'm telling you is false and designed to misguide you!"

He disguises and works in the shadows putting up a false front to deceive and ensnare. All false doctrines and cults have this quality. They may even sound plausible and may even sound like it is truth. He can't let you see the truth at a glance so it comes packaged in a different way. In this hour we live in, the number one problem we face is having false appear to us as real. This is why we must walk in discernment. It's amazing that now there is jewelry that looks so real that unless the person is trained they will think it's real. It shines like a diamond, is cut like a diamond therefore it must be a diamond until you let a trained jeweler look at it.

Years ago I was walking through an airport catching a flight to a meeting. A man walks up to me smiling with a pleasant demeanor and offers me a flower. Then he begins to talk to me and it sounded good.

"Man is God's creation," he said. "Love is a wonderful thing."

Being in a hurry I said, "I don't mean to be rude but I serve the Lord Jesus Christ."

He smiles and replies, "I believe in Jesus."

Now that sounds good and to an untrained person it sounds like we are on the same page. However I knew what group he belonged to and I was a little familiar with his beliefs. Yes he believed in Jesus. He believed that he was a good man and prophet and a great teacher but in their belief he is not the Son of God nor is Salvation obtained through Him. So to cut it short I told him that I believe in Jesus the Son of God, virgin born, that spilt His blood for my redemption and that He is the only way of Salvation. All of a sudden he seemed to be needed somewhere else. It sounded the same but it was not the same. The language even sounded the same but the meaning was not the same. Deception is deadly!

"But if our gospel be hid, it is hid to them that are lost: In whom the god of this world hath blinded the minds of them which believe not, lest the light of the glorious gospel of Christ, who is the image of God, should shine unto them. For we preach not ourselves, but Christ Jesus the Lord; and ourselves your servants for Jesus' sake. For God, who commanded the light to shine out of darkness, hath shined in our hearts, to *give* the light of the knowledge of the glory of God in the face of Jesus Christ." (2 Corinthians 4:3-6)

The word blind used here means to obscure. The enemy blinds the minds of men to the truth of the gospel. This is rampant in this hour that we live in. We were warned over and over again that strong delusion and deception would be released and we are seeing it raging in our world.

"Now the Spirit speaketh expressly, that in the latter times some shall depart from the faith, giving heed to seducing spirits, and doctrines of devils." (1 Timothy 4:1)

There will come a time that instructors with deceiving trapping lies will come and teach and instruct with doctrines that come from a devil god. Oh this is so true for this hour. A counterfeit truth and false damnable lies that lead people to false belief is very much on the scene. Many are thinking, 'It sounds so right, so lovely, so understanding and so easy. Why isn't there many ways to God? It doesn't matter what I believe as long as I believe something. Oh I believe that God is real. Aren't we all on the same road of spiritual enlightenment? Isn't it narrow-minded to believe there is just one way? Aren't there other books than the bible that teach other ways?'

These are lies from the very bowels of hell to deceive men from the truth of the Gospel and the falsehood goes on and on.

"I marvel that ye are so soon removed from him that called you into the grace of Christ unto another gospel: Which is not another; but there be some that trouble you, and would pervert the gospel of Christ. But though we, or an angel from heaven, preach any other gospel unto you than that which we have preached unto you, let him be accursed. As we said before, so say I now again, If any *man* preach any other gospel unto you than that ye have received, let him be accursed. For do I now persuade men, or God? or do I seek to please men? for if I yet pleased men, I should not be the servant of Christ." (Galatians 1:6-10 (KJV)

The Apostle Paul made no quarter with the enemy. What he said actually is let them be damned! Our translations say accursed! He did not waver. Let me give you some truths that are not debatable or open to change. Any teaching that denies the deity of Jesus, the virgin birth, the Blood of Jesus is not necessary for redemption, the resurrection or any teaching that denies that Jesus is the only way of Salvation is not a biblical, sound teaching and is a lie from the mouth of satan. Any of those things listed that are denied or refused in the "gospel" being presented is not truth. It is a counterfeit gospel.

As I was reading about the Civil War, I came across an encounter that happened to the Union Army. They were advancing on what is referred to as the Peninsula Campaign under General George McClellan. His force numbered around 75,000 men and across from him was a Confederate force of less than 25,000. General McClellan could have stormed forward on his way to Richmond to capture the Confederate Capital and possibly bring a swift end to the war before it waged on for several more years. The Confederate leader however had a plan: he had his men light several extra campfires, and spread them out and then had a group of soldiers get behind some trees and then march across the field and go over behind another group of trees. A little while later he would command them do the very same thing in the opposite direction. This he did a number of times to make it appear as though a vast army was waiting. He did this knowing that McClellan was observing everything. The reason is he knew him. He also knew another reason why this would work, which brings us to another tactic the enemies uses against us. It is fear!

Though McClellan was a brilliant organizer, administrator, and trainer of men, he had been called a "Young

Napoleon" and he had a weakness that kept him from attacking. Fear! Though he out numbered the enemy, he had the tendency to believe false intelligence and exaggerate the size of the Confederate Army. The Confederate leader knew this and played on that weakness within him. Abraham Lincoln said of McClellan that if he sent him 20,000 more troops he would still not go forward and would send word he needed 10,000 more by in the morning.

The enemy is a master at using fear to paralyze us. There is a saying that FEAR is False Evidence Appearing Real. Fear is the opposite of faith. You cannot walk in fear and faith at the same time. So the enemy knows if he can get you to operate in fear he has got you. Just as faith attracts so too fear attracts. It is a spiritual force. We cannot afford to walk in fear!

"For God did not give us a spirit of timidity (of cowardice, of craven and cringing and fawning fear), but [He has given us a spirit] of power and of love and of calm *and* well-balanced mind *and* discipline *and* self-control." (2 Timothy 1:7 AMP)

Fear is not of God. How many times did God say in His Word that we are to fear not! We cannot afford to give into fear. We have to stand in faith.

"Herein is our love made perfect, that we may have boldness in the day of judgment: because as he is, so are we in this world. There is no fear in love; but perfect love casteth out fear: because fear hath torment. He that feareth is not made perfect in love." (1 John 4:17-20)

When we understand the magnitude of God's love for us we do not have to fear. God knows your name, your cares, and your needs. He watches over you. He has a plan and purpose for your life. You don't need to walk in fear.

Notice that along with fear comes torment. God has never planned for you to live in torment. Have you ever looked to see how many phobias there are? There are too many to name here but people let their fear grow unchecked till it reaches a stage where they are trapped and controlled by their fear. Don't tolerate it! Get it out of your mind and heart. Remember Job? Notice what he said. He was a righteous man but notice he allowed fear to operate in his life.

"For the thing which I greatly fear comes upon me, and that of which I am afraid befalls me." (Job 3:25 AMP)

Job had fear concerning his children; he made sacrifices every day because he feared in regards to them. Search your heart and make sure this avenue in your life is shut down. Refuse to fear! Where does this battle take place? Let's look at the next tactic of the enemy; your thoughts.

One strategy of battle is to get the high ground. In our lives that high ground is our minds and our thoughts. This is also one of the key areas the enemy works.

"For as he thinketh in his heart, so *is* he." (Proverbs 23:7)

"Therefore I say unto you, Take no thought for your life, what ye shall eat, or what ye shall drink; nor yet for your body, what ye shall put on. Is not the life more than meat, and the body than raiment? Behold the fowls of the air: for they sow not, neither do they reap, nor gather into barns; yet your heavenly Father feedeth them. Are ye not much better than they? Which of you by taking thought can add one cubit unto his stature? And why take ye thought for raiment? Consider the lilies of the field, how they grow; they toil not, neither do they spin: And yet I say unto you, That even Solomon in all his glory was not arrayed like one of these. Wherefore, if God so clothe the grass of the field, which to day is, and to morrow is cast into the oven, *shall he* not much more *clothe* you, O ye of little faith? Therefore take no thought, saying, What shall we eat? or, What shall we drink? or, Wherewithal shall we be clothed? (For after all these things do the Gentiles seek:) for your heavenly Father knoweth that ye have need of all these things. But seek ye first the kingdom of God, and his righteousness; and all these things shall be added unto you. Take therefore no thought for the morrow: for the morrow shall take thought for the things of itself. Sufficient unto the day *is* the evil thereof." (Matthew 6:25-34)

Your thoughts control you. What you think on drives you. What you meditate on is what you are drawn to.

What is worry? It is meditating and thinking on the wrong things. The enemy does his best to influence and make you think on the wrong things. When you worry, you magnify the problem! You must take control of the way you think. You must guard the high ground for it is crucial.

"Casting down imaginations, and every high thing that exalteth itself against the knowledge of God, and bringing into captivity every thought to the obedience of Christ." (2 Corinthians 10:5)

What we must do is refuse to meditate on the negatives that the enemy puts in our thoughts. We have to bring it down. We have to make sure our thought life lines up with the truth of God's Word in every area.

"Be careful for nothing; but in every thing by prayer and supplication with thanksgiving let your requests be made known unto God. And the peace of God, which passeth all understanding, shall keep your hearts and minds through Christ Jesus. Finally, brethren, whatsoever things are true, whatsoever things *are* honest, whatsoever things *are* just, whatsoever things *are* pure, whatsoever things *are* lovely, whatsoever things *are* of good report; if *there be* any virtue, and if *there be* any praise, think on these things." (Philippians 4:6-8)

If you want the peace of God to rule in your life then you have to think correctly and according to His Word. Be sure you look at this area in your life. Scripture says that the peace of God will keep (mount guard; hem in; protect) your hearts and minds. Can you see the power of correct thinking? This is where many lose the battle. Meditate on the Word of God and let it saturate your heart and mind so that when the enemy brings a thought you can judge it by the Word and not be ensnared.

In the Civil War, the Confederate Army had marched to the point that they could see the Capital being built in Washington. They came to rest on Munson's Hill. The Union Army that was in charge of guarding Washington came out to stop the Confederates. As they charged up the hill of course the enemy fired upon them and they would retreat. Not only were the soldiers of the Confederacy there but also the artillery was impressive though they hadn't fired a shot at them from the huge cannon that rested upon the hill. This went on for nearly a month. The Union Army would storm the hill then be driven back.

One morning the Union Army woke up and behold the Confederate Army had left during the night. Gone, vanished in the night and they didn't even take the cannon. Well they rushed up the hill elated at their victory of holding off the Confederate Army and now they had a great spoil to keep which was the massive cannon that had rested at the top of the hill though it was never fired at them. This tool of death and destruction that had been aimed at them threatening to belch forth its deadly missile, this great spoil of victory, this sword if you will that hung over their head upon closer examination turned out to be nothing but a painted log! The Confederate Army had taken a huge log and painted it black and then leaned wagon wheels against it to make it resemble a cannon. They did this several times in the war to deceive the Union Army into thinking they had massive armaments in place when in all actuality there were none. These were called Quaker Guns.

What deceiving lies and thoughts has the enemy used to make you cower in fear and dread? Things which appeared to be true but in all actuality they weren't true. When we stop and think about the ways that we have allowed the enemy to hold us captive when instead we could have risen up and taken the victory, it is astounding. How long has he had a Quaker gun pointed at you?

Chapter 4

Our Redemption

It is very critical in our ability to wage a successful campaign in this warfare to grasp the power and the full extent of our redemption. The standard of measure used to describe the power of God in the Old Testament was the "Exodus." When the scripture would refer to God's saving and delivering power it mentions this event. This was the measuring stick to show the power of God. While powerful and mighty, that is not our standard of measure.

In the New Testament when it refers to the power of God it takes us to a new measuring device – the resurrection of the Lord Jesus. This was the new way to describe the power and extent of our deliverance. Think about how thrilling it is to ponder and hear about Moses, Egypt, the signs and wonders that were done as God led them from bondage. There was the crossing of the Red Sea, the Egyptians who were drowned and all of the miracles in the wilderness. Though these things are wonderful they can not compare with our deliverance, in fact they pale in significance. One of the biggest errors in the Body of Christ is when we always consider the things in the Old Testament as the standard of measure. Our Covenant is better, our deliverance is more powerful, our High Priest is better and even the Glory of the Old Testament cannot compare with the Glory of the New Testament. This is not to belittle or minimize the significance of the Old Testament at all. It is important to realize what redemption has done for you! It is glorious!

The definition of the word Redeem means to regain possession of by paying a price, to recover, to pay off, to receive back and satisfy as a promissory note. What a powerful word! So rich in meaning! Now let's consider the word Redeemer. A Redeemer is one who redeems. A final word to consider is Redemption, which is the act of redeeming, the recovery of what is mortgaged or pledged, the payment of a debt or obligation or the paying of the value of the note or property.

Here is the story of Redemption: God created His most valued possession, which was man, and placed him in the garden where he was to reign, subdue, and replenish the earth with his wife Eve. Through an act of deception Adam gave up his reign of this earth and handed it over to a fallen angelic being who then usurped the authority and therefore God's highest creation was in bondage to this despot of a ruler and this whole world system came under his control and dominion. Along with that he now laid claim to the souls of men who were now born under his dominion. God now was faced with the necessity of restoring man to his rightful place and to do that God must fulfill what the cost was, in order to redeem mankind back to Himself. The solution was to send a man, for a man lost it and therefore a man must gain it back. This had to be a man born out of satan's dominion and a man born as Adam was created. This man was Jesus (Redeemer) – born connected to the Father – born of a virgin not being the seed of man but the Seed of God, born out from under satan's control. Jesus was sent to bring man back into proper alignment through His death and resurrection – paid the full price of the note that stood over mankind. He paid it in full and therefore brought man Redemption and totally paid the note against man by His Blood!

"Christ hath redeemed us from the curse of the law, being made a curse for us: for it is written, Cursed *is* every one that hangeth on a tree: That the blessing of Abraham might come on the Gentiles through Jesus Christ; that we might receive the promise of the Spirit through faith." (Galatians 3:13-15)

"Forasmuch as ye know that ye were not redeemed with corruptible things, *as* silver and gold, from your vain conversation *received* by tradition from your fathers; But with the precious blood of Christ, as of a lamb without blemish and without spot:" (1 Peter 1:18-19)

"And I beheld, and, lo, in the midst of the throne and of the four beasts, and in the midst of the elders, stood a Lamb as it had been slain, having seven horns and seven eyes, which are the seven Spirits of God sent forth into all the earth. And he came and took the book out of the right hand of him that sat upon the throne. And when he had taken the book, the four beasts and four *and* twenty elders fell down before the Lamb, having every one of them harps, and golden vials full of odours, which are the prayers of saints. And they sung a new song, saying, Thou art worthy to take the book, and to open the seals thereof: for thou wast slain, and hast redeemed us to God by thy blood out of every kindred, and tongue, and people, and nation; And hast made us unto our God kings and priests: and we shall reign on the earth." (Revelation 5:6-10)

"God, who at sundry times and in divers manners spake in time past unto the fathers by the prophets, Hath in these last days spoken unto us by *his* Son, whom he hath appointed heir of all things, by whom also he made the worlds; Who being the brightness of *his* glory, and the express image of his person, and upholding all things by the word of his power, when he had by himself purged our sins, sat down on the right hand of the Majesty on high;" (Hebrews 1:1-3)

"But we see Jesus, who was made a little lower than the angels for the suffering of death, crowned with glory and honour; that he by the grace of God should taste death for every man." (Hebrews 2:9)

"Forasmuch then as the children are partakers of flesh and blood, he also himself likewise took part of the same; that through death he might destroy him that had the power of death, that is, the devil; And deliver them who through fear of death were all their lifetime subject to bondage. For verily he took not on *him the nature of* angels; but he took on *him* the seed of Abraham. Wherefore in all things it behoved him to be made like unto *his* brethren, that he might be a merciful and faithful high priest in things *pertaining* to God, to make reconciliation for the sins of the people." (Hebrews 2:14-18)

"And you *hath he quickened,* who were dead in trespasses and sins; Wherein in time past ye walked according to the course of this world, according to the prince of the power of the air, the spirit that now worketh in the children of disobedience: Among whom also we all had our conversation in times past in the lusts of our flesh, fulfilling the desires of the flesh and of the mind; and were by nature the children of wrath, even as others. But God, who is rich in mercy, for his great love wherewith he loved us, Even when we were dead in sins, hath quickened us together with Christ, (by grace ye are saved;)" (Ephesians 2:1-5)

"And no man hath ascended up to heaven, but he that came down from heaven, *even* the Son of man which is in heaven. And as Moses lifted up the serpent in the wilderness, even so must the Son of man be lifted up: That whosoever believeth in him should not perish, but have eternal life. For God so loved the world, that he gave his only begotten Son, that whosoever believeth in him should not perish, but have everlasting life. For God sent not his Son into the world to condemn the world; but that the world through him might be saved. He that believeth on him is not condemned: but he that believeth not is condemned already, because he hath not believed in the name of the only begotten Son of God." (John 3:13-19)

These are only a small portion of the hundreds of Scripture that show us our redemption and the value of man that God was willing to pay to redeem and restore him. This is the Good News; the Gospel. We have been redeemed and restored! We have been put back in proper alignment with our heavenly Father. This is called Sonship! This should cause a praise to erupt from the very depths of your heart and soul. Think of His love for you, the sacrifice paid for you, and the penalty that was paid. The note is now...PAID IN FULL!

"And you, being dead in your sins and the uncircumcision of your flesh, hath he quickened together with him, having forgiven you all trespasses; Blotting out the handwriting of ordinances that was against us, which was contrary to us, and took it out of the way, nailing it to his cross;" (Colossians 2:13-15)

"And you who were dead in trespasses and in the uncircumcision of your flesh (your sensuality, your sinful carnal nature), [God] brought to life together with [Christ], having [freely] forgiven us all our transgressions, having cancelled *and* blotted out *and* wiped away the handwriting of the note (bond) with its legal decrees *and* demands which was in force *and* stood against us (hostile to us). This [note with its regulations, decrees, and demands] He set aside *and* cleared completely out of our way by nailing it to [His] cross." (Colossians 2:13-14 AMP)

Not only was the note paid, the very note is gone, with no evidence it existed. That is what was done through the cross and the resurrection. Isn't that powerful? It would be like struggling to pay your mortgage, then someone pays it off and gives you the title and when you go to the bank they can't find a note ever existed. Wouldn't you shout over that? That is exactly what took place in our redemption.

This is such a wonderful thing and I'm so thankful God redeemed us. What we need to understand is there are two aspects of Calvary and the Resurrection. There is the side that deals with our redemption and the cost of it but there is one aspect we need to understand just as well if we are to wage successful warfare. That is the side of it that dealt with satan's power and authority. If we do not grasp this aspect of it we will not walk in the victory of our redemption as God intended.

Jesus absolutely demolished the kingdom of darkness in the spirit realm. It was a spiritual D-Day. The enemy thought he had won. This man that had challenged him and disrupted his plans; this man that caused his little demons to tremble and beg for mercy; this man that had caused disease to leave bodies and blind eyes opened; this man that even raised some from the clutches of death; this man that was heralded as a Messiah and King he now thought was in his grasp. Yes he had been difficult to handle but now this miracle worker lay in the clutches of death. He mused to himself, thinking 'As usual I have proven to be the most powerful.' Hearing the laughter and jeers of the demonic imps rejoicing in their victory, he was beginning to smirk at the thought of this defeated challenger when suddenly a rumble began to shake the foundations of hell and light was penetrating the darkness.

If satan had known what was going to happen he would not have pushed so hard to incite the plan in the hearts of man. He did not know that he had signed his own death warrant.

"But we speak the wisdom of God in a mystery, *even* the hidden *wisdom*, which God ordained before the world unto our glory: Which none of the princes of this world knew: for had they known *it*, they would not have crucified the Lord of glory." (1 Corinthians 2:7-9)

Satan did not see it coming! His plan was backfiring in his face. You see he is not anything like God. He is not omnipotent (all-powerful), omniscient (all-knowing) neither is he omnipresent (every where at once) .We have believed the lies and falsehoods. The following Scriptures will allow us a look at what Calvary and the Resurrection did to him.

"That the God of our Lord Jesus Christ, the Father of glory, may give unto you the spirit of wisdom and revelation in the knowledge of him: The eyes of your understanding being enlightened; that ye may know what is the hope of his calling, and what the riches of the glory of his inheritance in the saints, And what *is* the exceeding greatness of his power to us-ward who believe, according to the working of his mighty power, which he wrought in Christ, when he raised him from the dead, and set *him* at his own right hand in the heavenly *places*, Far above all principality, and power, and might, and dominion, and every name that is named, not only in this world, but also in that which is to come: And hath put all *things* under his feet, and gave him *to be* the head over all *things* to the church, which is his body, the fulness of him that filleth all in all." (Ephesians 1:17-23)

"*And* having spoiled principalities and powers, he made a shew of them openly, triumphing over them in it." (Colossians 2:15)

"And being found in fashion as a man, he humbled himself, and became obedient unto death, even the death of the cross. Wherefore God also hath highly exalted him, and given him a name which is above every name: That at the name of Jesus every knee should bow, of *things* in heaven, and *things* in earth, and *things* under the earth; And *that* every tongue should confess that Jesus Christ *is* Lord, to the glory of God the Father." (Philippians 2:8-11)

"But every man in his own order: Christ the firstfruits; afterward they that are Christ's at his coming. Then *cometh* the end, when he shall have delivered up the kingdom to

God, even the Father; when he shall have put down all rule and all authority and power. For he must reign, till he hath put all enemies under his feet. The last enemy *that* shall be destroyed *is* death." (1 Corinthians 15:23-26)

"And Jesus came and spake unto them, saying, All power is given unto me in heaven and in earth. Go ye therefore, and teach all nations, baptizing them in the name of the Father, and of the Son, and of the Holy Ghost: Teaching them to observe all things whatsoever I have commanded you: and, lo, I am with you alway, *even* unto the end of the world. Amen." (Matthew 28:18-20)

"I *am* he that liveth, and was dead; and, behold, I am alive for evermore, Amen; and have the keys of hell and of death." (Revelation 1:18)

As we can see by these Scriptures, Jesus bound up the strongman and took back what rightfully belonged to God and restored to man what was taken by deception. We must understand that in the spirit realm, Jesus broke the power of the enemy. Jesus is absolute Lord of Lords and King of Kings!

We must come to understand the concept of what was done and what will be. Jesus' victory in the spirit realm is law, it is done! He is the victor. That's why when confronted in the spirit realm satan knows he is defeated and must bow at the name of Jesus. Every being in the spirit realm acknowledges who Jesus is. We have to enforce this in the earth. We must understand that all though it is done in the spirit realm, there is still an appointed time where satan's influence on this earth will continue.

We must stand and enforce the defeat that occurred, in this earthly realm. Satan knows his time with this earth is limited and that is one reason he is waging warfare at an intensified rate. God has bound Himself to His word. For the believer, satan's lordship is broken, for we walk in the Kingdom of Light. We are no longer in bondage to satan's rule. We operate in the laws that govern the Kingdom of

Light. We stand and declare the victory and freedom that we are called into. In the circumstances of our lives we declare what is legally ours in terms of the Covenant. Satan has been judged; and he is like an outlaw on the run. He knows his day of reckoning is fast approaching. In the natural realm the Redemption has not been made complete but it shall be. In the meantime we as soldiers in the Kingdom begin to take back that which the enemy has taken. We march forward in the victory that has been accomplished. God has broken the rulership of the enemy!

When we realize the intent and purpose of the ministry of Jesus we can see how masterful the strategy of the cross was by God. The purpose of the coming of Jesus.

"He that committeth sin is of the devil; for the devil sinneth from the beginning. For this purpose the Son of God was manifested, that he might destroy the works of the devil. The first Messianic prophecy given concerning Jesus was God's edict of war." (1 John 3:8)

"And I will put enmity between thee and the woman, and between thy seed and her seed; it shall bruise thy head, and thou shalt bruise his heel." (Genesis 3:15)

Jesus coming to earth and his death and resurrection had more ramifications than just salvation for man. It included that but it was the overthrow of Satan's dominion. The cross was a masterful military strategy; God used satan's own evilness against him by using the cross to swing the final blow to his kingdom. Satan pulled the trigger on the gun pointed at his own head. What the enemy saw as vulnerability actually contained God's masterful wisdom. Now the Body of Christ must walk forward in that victory. March on!

Chapter 5

Enforcing the Victory

When faced with the reality of what was accomplished through the cross and the Resurrection we find the truth of the call and purpose of the Church! We see the full scope of the Redemption and the role that we play in the enforcing of the victory that Jesus won at Calvary.

It is imperative that we understand what was provided for us in the Redemption and our position in Christ in light of it. We need to understand the done work of Calvary and the Resurrection. We also need to understand what is yet to be accomplished. Done is the fact that Jesus is already the Victor and He has already spoiled principalities and powers. Legally in the spirit realm it is already done. The yet to be factor is that although this is already accomplished we enforce the victory while here on this earth because satan is still operating in the earth. Creation has not yet had its redemption. The earth's system is still under the influence of satan and is dominated by him since the fall. He has already been judged and he has been stripped of his power and he is already defeated. God gave satan a time period to continue to reign until the appointed time and until all of creation is Redeemed.

When D-Day occurred in World War II, Hitler's fall already had begun. It wasn't until V-Day, the day of Victory that the war was ultimately over. Calvary is just like D-Day. That was the day of the invasion. In the spirit realm it is already passed and it is already accomplished. What we do in the meantime is we march forth and begin to enforce that victory. In other words when I am trying to receive a healing I stand on the fact that I am already healed. I stand on the position that I am not taking this ground back. It is already mine. Healing is already mine. It is not that I am trying to obtain it; it is that it is already bought, accomplished and finished. In this world even though judgment has been passed, satan is an outlaw and yet has a period of time that he is operating until God's appointed time and then satan's power is completely over. This is why Jesus said all authority has been given to us in heaven and in earth. This is why satan has to bow to the name of Jesus and this is why satan has to bow to the word. There is the established fact in the spirit realm of the Lordship of Jesus. There is however the total fulfillment yet to take place and that is where the Body of Christ finds itself in this hour.

The scripture is very clear on this subject when it states in Psalms 110:1: "The LORD said unto my Lord, Sit thou at my right hand, until I make thine enemies thy footstool."

Jesus applies this verse to Himself several times in the Gospels. (Mt. 12:44, Mk. 12:36, Lk. 20:43) He acknowledged the work that he would accomplish as well as the time of the full manifestation that would come. The writers of the New Testament understood this as well. Note the following Scriptures that bring this all to our understanding:

"Men and brethren, let me freely speak unto you of the patriarch David, that he is both dead and buried, and his sepulchre is with us unto this day. Therefore being a prophet, and knowing that God had sworn with an oath to him, that of the fruit of his loins, according to the flesh, he would raise up Christ to sit on his throne; He seeing this before spake of the resurrection of Christ, that his soul was not left in hell, neither his flesh did see corruption. This Jesus hath God raised up, whereof we all are witnesses. Therefore being by the right hand of God exalted, and having received of the Father the promise of the Holy Ghost, he hath shed forth this, which ye now see and hear. For David is not ascended into the heavens: but he saith himself, The LORD said unto my Lord, Sit thou on my right hand, until I make thy foes thy footstool. Therefore let all the house of Israel know assuredly, that God hath made that same Jesus, whom ye have crucified, both Lord and Christ." (Acts 2:28-36)

"And he shall send Jesus Christ, which before was preached unto you: Whom the heaven must receive until the times of restitution of all things, which God hath spoken by the mouth of all his holy prophets since the world began. For Moses truly said unto the fathers, A prophet shall the Lord your God raise up unto you of your brethren, like unto me; him shall ye hear in all things whatsoever he shall say unto you." (Acts 3:20-22)

"But to which of the angels said he at any time, Sit on my right hand, until I make thine enemies thy footstool?" (Hebrews 1:13-14)

"Then cometh the end, when he shall have delivered up the kingdom to God, even the Father; when he shall have put down all rule and all authority and power. For he must reign, till he hath put all enemies under his feet. The last enemy that shall be destroyed is death." (1 Corinthians 15:24-27)

"Who is gone into heaven, and is on the right hand of God, angels and authorities and powers being made subject unto Him." (I Peter 3:22)

As we can see here from the Scriptures presented, the victory has been won. Now there must come the full manifestation of that victory. The Body of Christ must now carry on that ministry of Jesus and enforce the decisive victory that was won through the cross and resurrection. We are to demonstrate and enforce the redemption by word and actions. To do this we must understand our position in Him. When we grasp the fact of our redemption and where we are to walk in the authority of it, then it can totally change our lives. We will rise up as a mighty army going forth in the power of God, demolishing the strongholds of the enemy bringing that truth of redemption into the lives of others. This was part of the calling of the Apostle Paul:

"And when we were all fallen to the earth, I heard a voice speaking unto me, and saying in the Hebrew tongue, Saul, Saul, why persecutest thou me? it is hard for thee to kick against the pricks. And I said, Who art thou, Lord? And he said, 'I am Jesus whom thou persecutest. But rise, and stand upon thy feet: for I have appeared unto thee for this purpose, to make thee a minister and a witness both of these things which thou hast seen, and of those things in the which I will appear unto thee; Delivering thee from the people, and from the Gentiles, unto whom now I send thee, To open their eyes, and to turn them from darkness to light, and from the power of Satan unto God, that they may receive forgiveness of sins, and inheritance among them which are sanctified by faith that is in me." (Acts 26:14-18)

We have this same calling and message to turn people from darkness to light and from the power of satan unto God. This is our calling and all of this is possible because of our position in Jesus! One of the most exciting things to study is our place in Him. I pray that revelation knowledge will flow into your life as we look at this glorious truth!

"And you hath he quickened, who were dead in trespasses and sins; Wherein in time past ye walked according to the course of this world, according to the prince of the power of the air, the spirit that now worketh in the children of disobedience: Among whom also we all had our conversation in times past in the lusts of our flesh, fulfilling the desires of the flesh and of the mind; and were by nature the children of wrath, even as others. But God, who is rich in mercy, for his great love wherewith he loved us, Even when we were dead in sins, hath quickened us together with Christ, (by grace ye are saved;) And hath raised us up together, and made us sit together in heavenly places in Christ Jesus: That in the ages to come he might shew the exceeding riches of his grace in his kindness toward us through Christ Jesus. For by grace are ye saved through faith; and that not of yourselves: it is the gift of God: Not of works, lest any man should boast. For we are his workmanship, created in Christ Jesus unto good works, which God hath before ordained that we should walk in them." (Ephesians 2:1-10)

Notice that we have been raised up with Him! There is a great deal of significance in this. As far as God is concerned, we are already seated with Jesus at the throne.

"But God, so rich is He in His mercy! Because of and in order to satisfy the great and wonderful and intense love with which He loved us, Even when we were dead (slain) by [our own] shortcomings and trespasses, He made us alive together in fellowship and in union with Christ; [He gave us the very life of Christ Himself, the same new life with which He quickened Him, for] it is by grace (His favor and mercy which you did not deserve) that you are saved (delivered from judgment and made partakers of Christ's salvation). And He raised us up together with Him and made us sit down together [giving us joint seating with Him] in the heavenly sphere [by virtue of our being] in Christ Jesus (the Messiah, the Anointed One). He did this that He might clearly demonstrate through the ages to come the immeasurable (limitless, surpassing) riches of His free grace (His unmerited favor) in [His] kindness and goodness of heart toward us in Christ Jesus." (Ephesians 2:4-7 AMP)

This is the reality we must grasp: Our position "in Him". This, our position in Him, is already accomplished and it is not something we try to attain. Any revelation we receive can only be as powerful in our lives to the degree that we can comprehend it. Every facet of our walk with the Lord is governed by this fact of who we are "in Him". Our total life of victory starts at this position of being "seated with Him". From the beginning of our journey, we are to start out in the "seated" position. This is an attitude of rest and not a straining nor a struggle to attain. We learn to "walk" by being "seated". This is the progression we see in the book of Ephesians.

Our Position in Christ: Seated (Eph. 2:6) Enthroned with Him. He made us to be joined in His dominion.

Our Life in the World: Walk (Eph. 4:1) To conduct one's self, to order one's behavior. Through the power of the Holy Spirit within us we follow Him in a practical; holy life. The out working of our being seated "in Him"

Our Position against the enemy: Stand (Eph. 6:11) Hold your ground! Stand in the face of the attack of the enemy and do not relinquish what was bought for you and is your covenant right. We maintain and remain in the victory Jesus obtained.

Everything comes out of our being "in Him". We think if we get our walk right, we will grow to where we have the strength to defeat the enemy, but this is a wrong conception. We fail to understand that all we need is provided by our being "in Him" and what He has already done! Therein lies the secret! Our union with Him already puts at our disposal everything we need to reign. We don't have to strive to obtain for it is already given to us by Jesus and the work He did at the cross and His Resurrection. It is so very critical to our entire life that we understand how God views us, since we are now "in Him". The enemy fears you learning who you are in Jesus!

In Him we are: Joint – Heirs!

"The Spirit itself beareth witness with our spirit, that we are the children of God: And if children, then heirs;

heirs of God, and joint-heirs with Christ; if so be that we suffer with him, that we may be also glorified together." (Romans 8:16-17)

Joint heirs; we are made equal inheritors! Let the power of that sink into your thinking. This means we are sharing His inheritance with Him. Glory to God, we also share in that victory over the enemy!

In Him we are: Kings & Priests!

"Ye also, as lively stones, are built up a spiritual house, an holy priesthood, to offer up spiritual sacrifices, acceptable to God by Jesus Christ." (1 Peter 2:5)

"But ye are a chosen generation, a royal priesthood, an holy nation, a peculiar people; that ye should shew forth the praises of him who hath called you out of darkness into his marvellous light:" (1 Peter 2:9)

The word royal here is the translation of the Greek word for king. We are kings / priests to live in a way that is to manifest and show forth the victory of our King Jesus! The word Holy here means set apart for His service. The word peculiar does not mean strange or odd but here means to "make around"; that is to surround within a circle indicating ownership. So we have been made kings and priests, set apart for His service, encircled with the seal of His owner- ship because we were bought and redeemed by His blood!

In Him we are: Sons!

"For as many as are led by the Spirit of God; they are the sons of God. For ye have not received the spirit of bondage again to fear; but ye have received the Spirit of adoption, whereby we cry, Abba, Father. The Spirit itself beareth witness with our spirit, that we are the children of God:" (Romans 8:14-16)

The Holy Spirit places the children of God (tecknon: born ones) as adult sons in a legal standing before God and in their relationship with Him.

71

"Now I say, That the heir, as long as he is a child, differeth nothing from a servant, though he be lord of all; But is under tutors and governors until the time appointed of the father. Even so we, when we were children, were in bondage under the elements of the world: But when the fullness of the time was come, God sent forth his Son, made of a woman, made under the law, to redeem them that were under the law, that we might receive the adoption of sons. And because ye are sons, God hath sent forth the Spirit of his Son into your hearts, crying, Abba, Father. Wherefore thou art no more a servant, but a son; and if a son, then an heir of God through Christ." (Galatians 4:1-7)

The word child here speaks of one who is immature and is in need of one to guide him such as a legal guardian; until a certain time set by the father when the child (son) was placed or received into adult maturity or sonship! Even as a child a Prince is still a Prince and he is already a part of the Royal household. He does not have to be grafted into the family. There comes a day though when he will be introduced officially as Prince. There is no question that we all have to grow into maturity in the Lord in order to handle things in the wisdom of God. With great power comes great responsibility. Anointing without character is deadly. We must understand that we are not trying to get to a place where all of a sudden we are mature enough to be able to merit sonship, but that we are already a son in the household of faith. We are not trying to attain sonship for we are already sons. We must get the western world idea of adoption out of our minds for that is not what the writer had in mind. The earth, still in the clutches of the fall, awaits our maturing in Him and for us to step into our rightful place and enforce the Redemption.

"For the earnest expectation of the creature waiteth for the manifestation of the sons of God." Romans (8:19-20)

We are to go forward in the victory that was established and completed at the Cross and Resurrection. Jesus has already gained that victory and we move forward enforcing it. We are already seated with Him above the despicable demonic realm. We walk under an "open heaven" already in the light of redemption. While the enemy sets up strongholds in certain areas, we don't have to conduct this whole massive array of trying to pull down, bind and rebuke these things before the power of God can be demonstrated. We just take it by faith walking in the accomplished victory of Jesus.

For example, in the New Testament nowhere do we see Jesus stopping outside of a city and saying, 'Before we go in there and minister healing and deliverance we have to attack all these powers and principalities.'

Jesus, our perfect example, just went in and did what was ordained by the Father to do! Nowhere do we see the Apostles stopping before ministering in a city or country and having this massive warfare before ministering in the city. They just went in with the anointing of God and ministered healing, deliverance and taught the Gospel.

We have given the enemy too much power. It doesn't hurt to pray over a city or a country and God will at times instruct us to bind the enemy over a region or country. The point I am making is; if you think the power of the enemy is so strong that you cannot fulfill the great Commission without all this massive effort of so called warfare over a city, then you have not grasped the level of the victory Jesus has already accomplished and gave us who know Him, the same power and authority to do so.

In Him we are: More than Conquerors!

"Nay, in all these things we are more than conquerors through him that loved us. For I am persuaded, that neither death, nor life, nor angels, nor principalities, nor powers, nor things present, nor things to come, Nor height, nor depth, nor any other creature, shall be able to separate us from the love of God, which is in Christ Jesus our Lord." (Romans 8:36-39)

We are overcomers because we are "in Him" the Overcomer. "More than conquerors" is a phrase meaning more than victorious, to gain surpassing victory. We walk in the fruits of Jesus' victory.

"For if by one man's offence death reigned by one; much more they which receive abundance of grace and of the gift of righteousness shall reign in life by one, Jesus Christ." (Romans 5:17-18)

We reign in life! We move in our lives as the anointed; with the anointing of the Anointed One (Christ) flowing out of us. We march in that Victory making His enemies His footstool!

Chapter 6

Becoming a Warrior

If you stood outside a major training center such as Ft. Hood in Texas or Ft. Polk in Louisiana you would observe the arrival of fresh recruits getting off the bus. You would observe men and women of all ethnic backgrounds, all different shapes and sizes, those taken from various backgrounds and strata of life. There in the mixture of new recruits would be the rich, the poor and those from middle income families, there would be those with higher education and some that are dropouts. They each have different reasons for joining; some to take advantage of the benefits, some to develop a career, some just to escape the lives that they were raised in. However, one thing they have in common is they are raw recruits. They have stepped into un-chartered waters. When they stepped off that bus they no longer were in control of their lives. Self-will is about to be confronted and conquered! They will now be molded, shaped, trained. They will be called upon to change the way they think, they will become disciplined and focused. They will be called to a new level of sacrifice, courage, and boldness. They will confront their fears, overcome hindrances, find new talents and tap into new levels of reserve and fortitude they never knew was inside them. Warriors are not born; they are forged through training, discipline, battle and knowledge.

Doesn't this sound like the Body of Christ? God has called a group of people that are so varied and different. They come with different backgrounds, talents, abilities, and strengths, now recruited into the army of the Lord! No one is called into this army as an observer, to sit passively by and let the war pass them by as they sit out of harm's way. We are called to serve not sit!

As I write this I am reminded of a movie I once saw, where there were men who stepped onto the bus with determined purpose and they enlisted with purpose. Some were seemingly jolted with a slap of cold harsh reality with the wake-up call of a drill instructor shouting orders in their face wondering how they got there. It reminded me of those who have been saved but are clueless to the world they have just entered. They signed on as it were for heaven – not to fight. Yet they are suddenly awakened to the harsh reality of warfare and battle.

'What do you mean warfare? What battle? No one said anything about training and discipline!'

Welcome, my friend, you're in the Army now!

When you enlist, you are now the property of the Armed Services. You have just become a part of the war machine. Doesn't matter what you were before you arrived. You are now the sole property of them. They make no excuses while reminding you that you are no longer your "own individual" and that "free spirit of wanderlust" is now corralled, that "rebellious lone ranger" has hung up his saddle. From this moment on, you will be told what to eat, and when you will eat it, what to wear, how to make your bed, how to shine your shoes, when you will walk, when you will run, and you will be told when to go to bed and when you will get up.

You have just lost control! You can't dress the way you want, decide when to wake up or even what time you do anything. Now you will be drilled in such things as code, honor, integrity, discipline, order, hiking, marching, obstacles, and teamwork. Worst of all, these instructions will not be delivered to you by the soothing voice of your Mom who understands your "sensitive nature" or the consoling words of your Dad who understands that you have a total natural "abhorrence" to physical demands. Your charm will not work and your charismatic appeal is lost on these instructors. They aren't impressed with your accomplishments in the past or your position on the social ladder. They see one thing, a raw recruit that they must prod, mold, and train into a soldier. They aren't concerned with your viewpoint and they won't ask it. You are property to be trained and used! They won't care if they offend you. They know their job and the amount of time they have in which to accomplish it. What isn't seen is that they are highly aware of the fact that standing in front of them are future Generals, Lieutenants, Corporals, and that some will go into specialized fields such as Green Berets, Seals, and Airborne. There could possibly be a future President in their midst. It is their job to begin their training with efficiency and skill. They are to make you all that you can be.

We seem to have lost this concept of training and equipping within the Body of Christ. When we become born again we have just begun the journey. We are all raw recruits that are no longer the masters of our own lives. Today, some people seem to be put off with words like discipline, teamwork, code of honor, protocol, and commitment. They have their eyes on certain things, the office of General, the great dress uniform, the ability to lead others, and the medals yet they refuse to understand that they will have to start with Boot Camp. There is no other way. Regardless of how talented, gifted or anointed you may be – we all start here. Here is a secret you must understand: **You will never move in authority till you learn to be under authority!** Until you have learned to be trained and master certain skills, you will never rise to your full potential.

Paul said; "What? Know ye not that your body is the temple of the Holy Ghost *which is* in you, which ye have of God, and ye are not your own? For ye are bought with a price: therefore glorify God in your body, and in your spirit, which are God's." (1 Corinthians 6:19-20)

"Ye are bought with a price; be not ye the servants of men. Brethren, let every man, wherein he is called, therein abide with God." (1 Corinthians 7:23-24)

What I want you to see from these scriptures is that "Ye are not your own." Why is that? "You have been bought!"

We must help people to understand that when they surrender to the Lord they have to lay down ownership. I know in the age that we live in this is not a popular thought. It does not tickle the ears of people.

'Hey I just signed on to follow Jesus and not for all this training stuff. I don't need anyone to teach me anything, besides this is just the way I am.'

Sorry to burst your bubble but the truth is that you are going to have to change. Yes you have a free will and God will not railroad you into anything but you will never accomplish anything worthwhile unless you submit to the training that He has prepared for you. If you stay in that mindset you may make heaven but you will never have the impact, or accomplish anything of any degree without going through this process of training and equipping. When I confess Him as Lord, it means Lord over every area of my life. I must now be molded, and shaped into the vessel He desires. I don't own me anymore! You are no longer "master" of your life.

Paul gave us further insight: "Know ye not that they which run in a race run all, but one receiveth the prize? So run, that ye may obtain. And every man that striveth for the mastery is temperate in all things. Now they *do it* to obtain a corruptible crown; but we an incorruptible. I therefore so run, not as uncertainly; so fight I, not as one that beateth the air: But I keep under my body, and bring *it* into **subjection**: lest that by any means, when I have preached to others, I myself should be a castaway." (1 Corinthians 9:24-27)

My there is a word that we don't like subjection! In most circles that word brings a gasp of horror and recoil.

'Subjection? You have got to be kidding! Not me! Bondage never! I will not have that.'

Let's look at this word subjection: a Greek compound word doulous and ago meaning to be a slave driver; i.e. to enslave (subdue); bring into subjection.

'Surely this can't be! This sounds like bondage, control, discipline, like slavery!' Let's look for a different translation. Williams Translation of the word subjection: "but I keep on beating and bruising my body and making it my slave." Weymouth Trans: "I bruise my body and make it my slave "

Wait lets look at the same Scripture in the Amplified Bible and clear this up!

"But [like a boxer] I buffet my body [handle it roughly, discipline it by hardships] and subdue it, for fear that after proclaiming to others the Gospel *and* things pertaining to it, I myself should become unfit [not stand the test, be unapproved and rejected as a counterfeit]." (1 Corinthians 9:27 AMP)

'Oh no, Paul must not have completely understood. We are free! Why we aren't under Law but Grace. There are no rules or laws. God knows my heart. I don't have to change or conform to the Word. I'm free!'

Why would Paul say things like 'I'm a prisoner of the Lord,' or 'I am a bondservant of the Lord?' It is because Paul knew that his life was not his own. He gave up all his rights for self-government and strove to be conformed to the image of Christ. Many today are instead preaching a gospel of self-help and one of a please-me mentality. What is being presented is a gospel that excuses sin and self will, yet this is not at all what Paul preached.

Warriors are not born. They are molded and created through discipline, training, and hardship.

General Robert E. Lee said, "I must train them to be servants of their country by making them masters of themselves." Lee believed self-denial and self-control were keys to life. He believed there were two fundamentals of a soldier's life discipline and co-operation and without these key elements a soldier could not stand gallantly in battle.

This is where many miss it. It is easy in the excitement of victory to forget the training and discipline and planning that laid the foundation of the victory. War calls for preparation! Never forget that!

David said: "Blessed *be* the LORD my strength, which teacheth my hands to war, *and* my fingers to fight:" (Psalms 144:1-2)

King Solomon said: "*Every* purpose is established by counsel: and with good advice make war." (Proverbs 20:18)

"For by wise counsel thou shalt make thy war: and in multitude of counsellors *there is* safety." (Proverbs 24:6)

Training is essential! No one is ready to step onto the battlefield without it. Lack of training will cost you and can make you become a casualty instead of a victor. If you think you can fulfill your calling and destiny without it or that you can go your own way and do everything like you want to do it, then I say to you without hesitation you will fail! The enemy will pick you off as swiftly as he can. It is because you have made yourself an easy target!

Let's look at the men David was surrounded with. Notice how these are described in various verses throughout I Chronicles Chapter 12: They were ready, armed to the war (vs. 23). They were expert in war, with all instruments of war (vs.33). One of the most important, they could keep rank and were not of double heart (vs. 38).

Notice that even though David was anointed King there were certain things that he had come through and was known for. He had slain Goliath, he could worship God, and he had defeated the lion and the bear. Even the Prophet told of David's future greatness, but David could not do it alone or before God's timing. You see the lion and bear were training, for Goliath and the men surrounding David were disciplined, trained, skilled men. Allow this to sink into your heart and spirit.

There are some key areas that we will need to be trained in. Some of the training will seem mundane and you will perhaps at times wonder if this is all necessary. You may even wonder what it has to do with the battlefield.

I recall the story in the movie the Karate Kid. There are several lessons one could take from the movie. The boy wants to learn Karate to defend himself. He has seen the moves and the power of Karate. He approaches his friend, an older man, and asks him to teach him to fight and to teach him Karate. The wise old man instead directs him to paint the fence! The boy is shocked and does not understand and begins to angrily start slapping paint. The old man comes out and corrects him showing him the proper up and down movement that is required in order to paint correctly. Next, the boy once again approaches the old man and states that he is now ready and asks once again that he teach him to fight. This time the wise old instructor tells him to wash and wax cars. Now the boy is livid, spitting and sputtering and totally disgusted. Again he just starts doing it when the instructor comes out and shows him the proper way putting on the wax with one hand and taking off the wax with the other. When he finishes, he becomes angry and disgusted with the old man. He tells him how useless all that was. What a waste of time! He wanted to learn Karate! It is then that the old man begins to show him that the very moves he learned in the mundane tasks of painting the fence and waxing the cars were some of the basic moves he would use to defend himself with Karate.

Some of the training will appear elementary and as everyday basics. Some feel they are too far advanced to require this, yet they have not mastered the basics. One may think they are too trivial, failing to realize that this will be the foundation of victories to come.

It is in the fire of discipline, that habits and character are formed. The need to shape the raw material of these recruits is there. The necessity of the Boot Camp is to now form these various individuals into the mold of warriors.

Here is a scripture that bares learning and dedicating into your mindset:

"*He that is* slow to anger *is* better than the mighty; and he that ruleth his spirit than he that taketh a city." (Proverbs 16:32)

Lets look at this word ruleth: a primitive root; to *rule*: (have, make to have) dominion, governor, indeed, reign, (bear, cause to, have) rule (-ing, -r), have power.

What are some of the key elements a person learns in Boot Camp? What are some of the disciplines to be acquired? If we are to be forged into warriors fit to be used in battle then we need to see the importance of the following vital lessons from Boot Camp.

Lessons from Boot Camp: Obedience

One of the most critical areas learned is the capacity to hear an order and obey it. From the time a person enters the Armed Services they are barraged with commands that are expected to be obeyed immediately. Insubordination is not excusable at all. Orders are given and are not open to debate ones feelings or ones opinion. Through the drills given will be forged the quality of following commands without hesitation or delay. This quality can be a key that will possibly save your life on the battlefield. The instructors know this and with all diligence seek to instill this into every recruit.

This ability to follow orders promptly can make the difference between victory and defeat. Men must be trained to obey or they can not be controlled in battle.

Learning to obey the promptings of the Holy Spirit and the directions of the Word are absolutely necessary to be victorious in our Spiritual Warfare. I can say with full candor that if you fail to obey, it could cost you your life. We must learn the wisdom of obedience. It unlocks the doors to our victories. God will never promote you beyond your last act of disobedience. Until that last act of disobedience is rectified, you will be hindered in your growth and development.

"And Samuel said, Hath the LORD *as great* delight in burnt offerings and sacrifices, as in obeying the voice of the LORD? Behold, to obey *is* better than sacrifice, *and* to hearken than the fat of rams. For rebellion *is as* the sin of witchcraft, and stubbornness *is as* iniquity and idolatry. Because thou hast rejected the word of the LORD, he hath also rejected thee from *being* king." (1 Samuel 15:22-23)

God puts a high premium on obedience. Saul had his orders, yet he thought it would be better to amend them. He felt it would be okay to slightly change the order. While at times you may question commands or you may not even agree with them fully, let me persuade you to obey. Trust the orders whether they are given by the Word or through the prompting of the Holy Spirit. God was not delighted at all with Saul's partial obedience because what He expected was total obedience.

God despises, hates and will judge swiftly acts of rebellion. Partial obedience is not total obedience, which God requires. One of the things God dealt so strongly with Israel was their disobedience. Time and time again they would chafe and rebel against the commands of God. He called them stiff-necked and rebellious. Here is the breakdown from God's viewpoint: rebellion equals witchcraft, stubbornness equals iniquity and idolatry. I believe it is clear to see the attitude of the Father.

'Wait a minute, isn't God loving, kind, longsuffering, gentle; doesn't He love me?'

The answer is yes, but rebellion He will not condone nor tolerate. He gives no quarter to intent or half- hearted obedience. We must learn the act of obedience. Many people have been defeated because they never learned the basics of obedience. They run their lives as if they have the right to live it as they choose; obeying only what they can agree with or accept. How many ministries have been aborted because they failed to learn this lesson? There have been churches and ministries birthed by rebellion. It will never grow or prosper because the foundation is wrong.

Let's look at Brother Foolish. He is saved and begins to follow the Lord and then he is called into the ministry. God wants him to sit under his Pastor and begin to be trained; the Pastor is a Godly man and does teach the Word of God accurately. Brother Foolish is content for a little while as the Pastor mentors him. The Pastor recognizes the calling on his life but also sees the areas that need to be trained and developed. Brother Foolish begins to think he is qualified, knows why God has called him, and thinks after all that he can even preach better than the Pastor and he would certainly do things different than the Pastor. Therefore, he begins to grow disgruntled and thinks the Pastor is just holding him back. Brother Foolish, instead of sitting and learning, being trained and developed, and without hearing clearly from the Lord on the timing of things, he decides it's time.

'I will start my own church,' he declares.

So he leaves with family, friends and the five people who compliment him every time he speaks and starts his own church.

Flash forward two years and either the doors are closed or he still has the twenty people that he started with. You see, if he had learned to sit and wait and be instructed, which is what God intended, if he had learned to be obedient to those over him for a season, then when the proper time came the Lord would have placed him where he needed to be and his work would have been fruitful. Yet this is how so many churches and ministries were birthed.

God however will never bless disobedience. I know that every person will go through these seasons. I know it may be hard at times to wait until the proper time but it is necessary. To move ahead in our own wisdom or our own timing could bring disaster. If the Lord requires you to stay in a place for a season then to move before the clear command would be disobedience. God would not have you stay where error is taught, or you were being abused and misused but He could require you to sit for a while in a place you think you have grown beyond. When we don't have a clear direction it is important to stay with your last order or command. Again, the key is learning to obey orders.

Lessons from Boot Camp: Endurance

One of the things experienced in Boot Camp is the hiking, marching, obstacle courses, and a great deal of physical training. The purpose of course is to get the recruits in shape and to build endurance. A person has to build this up in their life. No one leaps off their couch after years of inactivity and runs a marathon.

I remember once in college a few of my friends came over and we decided to play football. Several of us had played in high school and so we took the field. We ran, dove, blocked, leaped, and even made impressive runs with the ball. We were the magnificent players of our former years. We gathered back at my house laughing and kidding each other then we all watched a football game. In about an hour, we were sore and stiffening. I began to hurt in places I forgot was on my body. The next morning I would have given sworn testimony that during the night I was run over by two cement trucks and an elephant had sat on my legs.

In playing football, I remember the conditioning drills we went through. It wasn't fun! Honestly, after hours of this in the hot August two-a-day practices, we muttered under our breaths complaints about their seemingly inhumane treatment of us. We wanted to play football! We wanted to score touchdowns, tackle, run a kick-off back or catch a splendid pass and most of all wear our letter jackets and look impressive. Then of course, we endured the coach lecturing us on the importance of endurance. 'Easy for him to say,' we thought. He wasn't the one sweating, groaning and hurting and his side wasn't hurting with every breath. It was soon afterwards that we would be in a tight game and would find ourselves in the last quarter where we had to rally and push through the tiredness and the field conditions. Soon the reserve that we had built into ourselves would surface and we would rise up and move onward. By enduring all the conditioning we had created a reservoir within ourselves to draw from. It was at this moment that we were thankful for a coach that at first we did not understand.

Endurance is a quality that is necessary to become a warrior!

"But he that shall endure unto the end, the same shall be saved. And this gospel of the kingdom shall be preached in all the world for a witness unto all nations; and then shall the end come." (Matthew 24:13-14)

Endure: to *stay under* (*behind*), i.e. *remain*; figurative to *undergo*, i.e. *bear* (trials), *have fortitude, persevere*: - abide, endure, (take) patient (-ly), suffer, tarry behind. Jesus thought endurance was a trait necessary to be victorious.

Paul instructed Timothy: "Thou therefore endure hardness, as a good soldier of Jesus Christ. No man that warreth entangleth himself with the affairs of *this* life; that he may please him who hath chosen him to be a soldier." (2 Timothy 2:3-4)

Endure: to *undergo hardship*: - be afflicted, endure afflictions (hardness), suffer trouble.

Endurance is so very important. Without endurance victory will not come. I like how a friend of mine put it, "Endurance is the ability to outlast the trial or battle." Endurance is the ability to outlast the enemy. So many people have been taken off the battlefield because they lacked this quality. They let the enemy wear them down to the point they gave up or quit. Endurance had never been fully developed in their life. It has been amazing to me over the years to see the things that people have allowed to stop them from continuing in the things of God!

"Take [with me] your share of the hardships *and* suffering [which you are called to endure] as a good (first-class) soldier of Christ Jesus." (2 Timothy 2:3 AMP)

Paul had spoken from experience. "Are they Hebrews? so *am* I. Are they Israelites? so *am* I. Are they the seed of Abraham? so *am* I. Are they ministers of Christ? (I speak as a fool) I *am* more; in labours more abundant, in stripes above measure, in prisons more frequent, in deaths oft. Of the Jews five times received I forty *stripes* save one. Thrice was I beaten with rods, once was I stoned, thrice I suffered shipwreck, a night and a day I have been in the deep; *In* journeyings often, *in* perils of waters, *in* perils of robbers, *in* perils by *mine own* countrymen, *in* perils by the heathen, *in* perils in the city, *in* perils in the wilderness, *in* perils in the sea, *in* perils among false brethren; In weariness and painfulness, in watchings often, in hunger and thirst, in fastings often, in cold and nakedness. Beside those things that are without, that which cometh upon me daily, the care of all the churches." (2 Corinthians 11:22-27)

You may never be called upon to go through the things that Paul went through but you will certainly be put in situations that will require endurance. You will need the ability to outlast what comes your way.

Jeremiah the Prophet said: "If thou hast run with the footmen, and they have wearied thee, then how canst thou contend with horses? and *if* in the land of peace, *wherein* thou trustedst, *they wearied thee*, then how wilt thou do in the swelling of Jordan?" (Jeremiah 12:5)

In other words, if the little things cause you to grow weary, what are you going to do when the going really gets tough? Endurance is a toughness of mind, heart and spirit. It is a quality that causes you to press through the obstacles, pain, disappointment, and delays. Remember the old watch commercial? "It takes a licking and keeps on ticking." What a great symbol of endurance! Honestly without endurance you will be a victim. Not every battle is over in seconds, in fact, some can take days, months or even years. Your ability to endure will make the difference and you will then be able to "take a licking and keep on ticking!"

A course that is taught is "Survival." Imagine, you are dropped in an area of harsh conditions with limited supplies and all that you have is your skill and knowledge to see you through. To survive, you may be required to eat something unpleasant, drink water that you would not normally drink and to seek shelter in places you would never pick under normal circumstances. It's not a fun thought, is it? Let's see Disneyland or the wilderness? Not too many would enjoy choosing the latter.

There will be "wilderness" experiences scheduled for your life. These are not there to destroy you but to build endurance into your life. Even Jesus experienced the wilderness.

I know some would say to themselves, 'Well if you have enough faith you never will have to go there.'

Wrong! There will be places that you must walk through that will require you to develop endurance. God loves you enough that He knows what is necessary to develop you.

It will not kill, steal or destroy you but it will be a time of training. This is a fact of training. How you handle this time of training is critical to your ability to survive and become a victor.

Here is a clip of dialogue from the movie Rambo/First Blood during the scene where they are trying to capture him and Rambo's Colonel has arrived to help.

Sheriff Teasle: Whatever possessed God in heaven to make a man like Rambo?

Colonel Trautman: God didn't make Rambo, I made him! I don't think you understand. I didn't come to rescue Rambo from you. I came here to rescue you from him.

Sheriff Teasle: Well, we all appreciate your concern Colonel; I will try to be extra careful!

Colonel Trautman: I'm just amazed he allowed any of your posse to live.

Sheriff Teasle: Is that right?

Colonel Trautman: Strictly speaking, he slipped up. You're lucky to be breathing.

Sheriff Teasle: That's just great. Colonel, you came out here to find out why one of your machines blew a gasket!

Colonel Trautman: You don't seem to want to accept the fact you're dealing with an expert in guerrilla warfare, with a man who's the best, with guns, with knives, with his bare hands. A man who's been trained to ignore pain, ignore weather, to live off the land, to eat things that would make a billy-goat puke. In Vietnam his job was to dispose of enemy personnel. To kill! Period! Win by attrition. Well Rambo was the best.

Rambo was a trained warrior. He was a created killing machine. Rambo knew endurance. Let's look at a real life example from history.

In the Civil War, under the leadership of Stonewall Jackson he had his Troops march 175 miles in twelve days, and some of these men were barefooted. To get them into position they had to make this march. This march occurred at Fredericksburg sometime during December. Can you imagine marching 175 miles barefoot, the temperature cold and the terrain rough, not smooth and paved? It took great endurance!

In this day and time it is easy for people to look and to find excuses not to do things. We are good at singing "I'm a soldier in the army of the Lord," but how quick are we to turn around and make excuses about the simple things, like getting up and going to church or attending Bible study this week or even reading the Word like we should? It is shocking to me to observe some of the levels of dedication that we see observed in other religions and even cults. We pride ourselves on our beliefs but don't show half the dedication or endurance some of these are showing to pagan religions and untruth. It is time to get a toughness about us. Are we willing to sacrifice anything and everything to be a soldier of the cross? Are we ready to endure and outlast whatever the enemy throws at us because we are sold out and committed to the army of the Lord?

I believe it is important that not only do our hearts, minds and spirits have to be developed and kept tough and sharp; but also even our physical bodies need to be disciplined and taken care of with proper eating, exercising, and rest. No matter how anointed you are or how great the gifting of God on your life, if you neglect these areas you will suffer. The enemy loves to attack us when we are fatigued and run down. What good is all this knowledge and anointing if you are not physically able to go minister because of your health? We need to get our bodies in alignment in order to help us physically endure. Fatigue can cloud your judgment, expose your weaknesses, and make you acceptable to the attacks of the enemy.

Lessons from Boot Camp: Procedure

A recruit must learn the military mindset. He or she must learn the proper procedures according to the military and even proper protocol. Their way of thinking has to be changed and they must learn to think according to procedures. This must begin to happen instinctively. I remember an old adage: 'There is a right way and a wrong way and then there is the military way.' Once again this is an area where debate is not welcomed or asked for and it doesn't matter your level of intelligence or lack thereof. There is procedure and it must be learned. There is procedure for making the bed, proper stowing of gear, cleaning the barracks, shining your shoes, marching, and the list goes on and on. A recruit may often be stopped and asked, "Soldier what is the proper procedure for stowing your gear?" There is no point in offering your own opinion over how it should be stored. He didn't ask the soldier for his thoughts or feelings. What is procedure?

This is what is expected of us in the Army of the Lord. We need to know procedure. We have to adjust our thinking and bring it in line with what God desires. Where do we find procedure? It will be contained in the Word of God. It is our manual of war. Here we learn to think in line with our Commander-in-Chief. Here we learn to do things His way and with His methods. Here is where we learn Kingdom Policy and Procedure. God will never violate what He has already said in His word. He will never issue orders that are contrary to the truth that is in the Word. Sometimes we are in battle and need a specific command or strategy, however, the rule is to stay in the Word of God until you get a Word from God. When God speaks, trust the fact it will always line up with the written Word.

God is not the author of confusion. While God does clearly speak to us through the prophetic or personally within our spirit through that still small voice, if someone comes to tell me that they heard from God and it violates or goes against the written Word of God, I know that they obviously did not hear correctly. Knowing the Word as I do, I know the value that the Word puts on the covenant of marriage and on the home and family. If someone approached me saying that they heard God say to divorce my wife of 20 years and marry another because this person would be better suited to help me with my calling and ministry, I can take that word back to the written Word of God and easily understand that God would never say something like that. God's voice and heart, His concepts and laws, and His policies and procedures are recorded in that Word. Scripture tells us that His sheep know His voice. Do you know your Commander-in-Chief and what His voice would sound like well enough that when faced with the deception that the enemy will place in front of you, that you will still stand strong in what His written policies and procedures clearly state? We must cause our thinking and our every day walk to come into line with God's word.

There is discipline involved in the renewing of the mind and changing our mindsets to align with the Word of God. We must grow in that discipline to the point where every time we face a situation we instantly weigh it against our policy and procedure manual.

Paul wrote: "I beseech you therefore, brethren, by the mercies of God, that ye present your bodies a living sacrifice, holy, acceptable unto God, *which is* your reasonable service. And be not conformed to this world: but be ye transformed by the renewing of your mind, that ye may prove what *is* that good, and acceptable, and perfect, will of God." (Romans 12:1-2)

How are we transformed: By renewing our minds! What is the purpose of this transformation? So that we may prove (know) the good, acceptable, perfect will of God.

A person who says it is impossible to understand or know the will of God has just shown you their failure to read and understand the Policy and Procedure Manual of the Kingdom of God.

Paul spoke further of this process when he wrote, "That ye put off concerning the former conversation the old man, which is corrupt according to the deceitful lusts; And be renewed in the spirit of your mind; And that ye put on the new man, which after God is created in righteousness and true holiness." (Ephesians 4:22-25)

We come into the Kingdom through salvation and now must learn how to flow in line with it. The only way to do that and begin to understand the procedures and policies is through the renewing of the mind and by submitting to God and allowing Him to change, mold and reshape our mindset. Every area of our life is covered in that wonderful manual called the Bible. There is Kingdom Policy and Procedure on the topic of our very own thoughts.

"Casting down imaginations, and every high thing that exalteth itself against the knowledge of God, and bringing into captivity every thought to the obedience of Christ; and having in a readiness to revenge all disobedience, when your obedience is fulfilled." (2 Corinthians 10:5-6)

Policy: Everything that exalts itself against what we know to be true of God we tear down.

Procedure: Cast it down, take every thought captive! It did not say entertain it or be tolerant or be open-minded. If it goes against the Word of God and what is revealed about Him you are to deal with it according to procedure.

"Finally, brethren, whatsoever things are true, whatsoever things *are* honest, whatsoever things *are* just, whatsoever things *are* pure, whatsoever things *are* lovely, whatsoever things *are* of good report; if *there be* any virtue, and if *there be* any praise, think on these things. Those things, which ye have both learned, and received, and heard, and seen in me, do: and the God of peace shall be with you." (Philippians 4:8-9)

Policy: Things true, honest, just, pure, and lovely, of good report, have virtue, has praise think on them.

Procedure: If it doesn't contain these elements cast them down and change your focus. Make yourself think on these things.

When we begin to worry or allow our mind to be filled with ungodly thoughts, we can know that our thinking is not in line with policy and procedure. You can not walk in victory if you do not make your thinking align with the word of God. The enemy will be able to confuse you and deceive you if you don't renew your mind daily, as your manual states. A quick remedy when the wrong thoughts start to consume you is to get into the Word and find out what it says about your situation.

Lessons from Boot Camp: Teamwork

The skill of learning to work as a cohesive unit is very important. No matter how much fire power an army has, no matter the vast amount of soldiers that may be in it, without the discipline of learning to function and flow as a unit will still bring about defeat. As I have extensively studied the battles of the Civil War, one thing that really stood out was that though the Union had an advantage in the vastness of men and weapons, oftentimes they were defeated at the start of a battle because the men were not disciplined and lacked unity. Many of the regiments had never learned the art of maneuvering and taking position on the battlefield. They had not learned to flow in a smoothly functioning team. Sometimes when marching to take position, brigades were hindered waiting on other brigades to cross and march by. This delayed taking advantage of time and weaknesses of the enemy. Supplies were slow in reaching the army because the logistics and skills that were needed to move and supply such a vast army was something that was not coordinated and caused many delays. Even delays in the dispersion of rations and supplies to the men cost valuable time because of a lack of coordinated teamwork. This was especially true at the Battle of Manassas.

For an army to function properly every area must flow and do its part with speed and efficiency. It must work like a well-oiled machine. From the basics of supplies to coordinating a pinpoint strike with a missile every part must function. It takes a massive effort.

In the world of sports, you could be the best running back that ever came along with great speed, size, and the ability to weave and dodge tacklers, but without the linemen to block for you and open up holes to run through, what good is all that talent? Without the coach to design the plays and make the strategy for the game, your talent is worthless. Without the people to take care of the equipment you wear or the trainers to tape you properly so that your ankles are strengthened, exactly how well would you do?

For the Body of Christ to be the Army that it is called to be, teamwork is vital! Much to the chagrin of the church this has been lost on a lot of people. Have you ever noticed that even Jesus sent out the disciples in twos? God never meant for anyone in the Body of Christ to be a 'Lone Ranger'. Unity and cohesiveness, is as vital for the Body of Christ as it is for any natural army.

Here is the model for the New Testament Church or ministry. God will raise up a person with a vision and they, through life circumstances and many battles fought and won, through much training and equipping, will be assigned to a place appointed and confirmed by God. God will then surround this person with the people and the team that is needed in order to carry out that vision. No one person has everything and the simple fact is that we were created with the need to be connected. Anyone who thinks they can fulfill their calling alone with the attitude that they don't need anyone else has already set in motion their very own defeat. We need each other. Remember our manual describes us as 'a body' and not 'a finger'. A finger without a hand can do nothing. A hand without an arm can not maneuver nor can it work the fingers. This is why the enemy fights unity so hard. The power that is found in unity is a mighty thing.

"I therefore, the prisoner of the Lord, beseech you that ye walk worthy of the vocation wherewith ye are called, with all lowliness and meekness, with longsuffering, forbearing one another in love; Endeavoring to keep the unity of the Spirit in the bond of peace. *There is* one body, and one Spirit, even as ye are called in one hope of your calling; One Lord, one faith, one baptism, One God and Father of all, who *is* above all, and through all, and in you all. But unto every one of us is given grace according to the measure of the gift of Christ. Wherefore he saith, when he ascended up on high, he led captivity captive, and gave gifts unto men. (Now that he ascended, what is it but that he also descended first into the lower parts of the earth? He that descended is the same also that ascended up far above all heavens, that he might fill all things.) And he gave some, apostles; and some, prophets; and some, evangelists; and some, pastors and teachers; For the perfecting of the saints, for the work of the ministry, for the edifying of the body of Christ: Till we all come in the unity of the faith, and of the knowledge of the Son of God, unto a perfect man, unto the measure of the stature of the fullness of Christ: That we *henceforth* be no more children, tossed to and fro, and carried about with every wind of doctrine, by the sleight of men, *and* cunning craftiness, whereby they lie in wait to deceive; But speaking the truth in love, may grow up into him in all things, which is the head, *even* Christ: From whom the whole body fitly joined together and compacted by that which every joint supplieth, according to the effectual working in the measure of every part, maketh increase of the body unto the edifying of itself in love." (Ephesians 4:1-17)

We see here that the five-fold ministry is given to the body to equip the body. It is designed to instruct and lead the body into maturity. This is why it is so important for these ministries to acknowledge one another and flow together. Any leader who is alone is not complete. Making decisions solely, in and of themselves and without accountability and responsibility to the rest of the team that the Lord has sent in, they will find that they somehow were just not enough. It is not a dictatorship and a true leader doesn't have to fight to maintain his role of authority. When working under the concepts of the manual and under the perfect way that God Himself could only design it, we find success in the Body of Christ and within each unit of the Army of the Lord. We have to have the offices of the five-fold ministry functioning and flowing together with unity, integrity, and accountability all the while understanding and acknowledging the giftings of each one.

It is just as necessary for each member (joint) to function in his or her proper place. One of the things that hinder the Body from being the mighty force it should be is people not discovering their function or giftings and then flowing in it.

It was never God's intention to "float" people from one place to another. I have been amazed over the years at how so many people have misunderstood this principle. It is important to clearly hear your instructions from the Commander-in-Chief (God) and to allow His confirming voice to instruct you on where to serve. God is not double-minded and is not the author of confusion. He never instructed anyone to go from church to church, never putting down any roots. His plan is for each person to pray and seek Him, receive His instruction as to where to go and then once that is settled to then begin to grow and develop and function in their place helping to co-labor and to build the vision while advancing the Kingdom. In due time, the Lord may begin to give you more responsibility and perhaps where you have been serving was in all actuality a training ground and for a season. The day may come where He may appoint you elsewhere or even assign you to a different region but when that time comes, it will come with confirmation so that you will clearly know your next instructions. While you are called to serve in any way that you can and to allow God to continually refine you, it is important to never step ahead of His plans. He has the battle plan and it will be He who issues you marching orders if and when that time may come. While there will be many leaders in our lives and lessons are learned in serving, submitting and committing, one must also realize that respectfully, we are to listen to God's voice, even above man's voice.

There has been a great falling away from the church. Much of this falls on the leaders who didn't fully understand the manual or the concept of five-fold ministry and what it was designed to do. These are ones who fell short in their own humanity and allowed pride and religion to control and there is a great lack of integrity today in the churches. Many leaders, out of the hurt of their own wounds, could not even trust others to co-labor with them in the vision that God placed before them. The result was that many were wounded in the church and some who wanted to serve were not given an opportunity or were wounded while trying to serve. Without a true example to look to, the sheep were scattered.

There is also, in today's society, an entertain-me-attitude. Many people lack the understanding of commitment and could not fathom that God might call them to serve in the very small church on the corner who struggles in feeding the hungry, instead of the great big mega church who has the latest technology where all people of influence attend.

We see them instead of planting themselves traveling from church to church looking for the best entertainment.

When God calls you to a place He has you there for a purpose. You can't just change your assignment because you want to. Sometimes the assignment is not easy or sometimes not even very appealing but the fact is, it is not up to you, it is up to God. Everything that you go through is a stepping stone of training for the next level. While God Himself may be highly disappointed in the leadership where He has placed you, this very situation could be training you in key character traits of Jesus. It may be a place to serve but to also humble you. It may be a lesson to learn in respect and honor and it could very well be a place to train you in things that you may never have an opportunity to be trained in again, if you step out before your time. His ways are not our ways. His thoughts are not our thoughts, but do you trust your Commander enough to wait?

If a person is not functioning where they are supposed to be functioning it affects the entire Kingdom of God. Have you ever had a broken or dislocated toe? It is amazing how that one little toe can throw off your balance, your speed, your ability to run or even walk, yet it's just a toe but it affects your whole person.

"For as the body is one, and hath many members, and all the members of that one body, being many, are one body: so also *is* Christ. For by one Spirit are we all baptized into one body, whether *we be* Jews or Gentiles, whether *we be* bond or free; and have been all made to drink into one Spirit. For the body is not one member, but many. If the foot shall say, Because I am not the hand, I am not of the body; is it therefore not of the body? And if the ear shall say, Because I am not the eye, I am not of the body; is it therefore not of the body? If the whole body *were* an eye, where *were* the hearing? If the whole *were* hearing, where *were* the smelling? But now hath God set the members every one of them in the body, as it hath pleased him. And if they were all one member, where *were* the body? But now *are they* many members, yet but one body. And the eye cannot say unto the hand, I have no need of thee: nor again the head to the feet, I have no need of you. Nay, much more those members of the body, which seem to be more feeble, are necessary: And those *members* of the body, which we think to be less honourable, upon these we bestow more abundant honour; and our uncomely *parts* have more abundant comeliness. For our comely *parts* have no need: but God hath tempered the body together, having given more abundant honour to that *part* which lacked: That there should be no schism in the body; but *that* the members should have the same care one for another. And whether one member suffer, all the members suffer with it; or one member be honoured, all the members rejoice with it. Now ye are the body of Christ, and members in particular. And God hath set some in the church, first apostles, secondarily prophets, thirdly teachers, after that miracles, then gifts of healings, helps, governments, diversities of tongues. *Are* all apostles? *are* all prophets? *are* all teachers? *are* all workers of miracles? Have all the gifts of healing? do all speak with tongues? do all interpret? But covet earnestly the best gifts: and yet shew I unto you a more excellent way." (1 Corinthians 12:12-31)

I want you to pay attention to that one phrase we see here in this passage in verse 18: God sets the members in their place as it pleases Him.

"But as it is, God has placed *and* arranged the limbs *and* organs in the body, each [particular one] of them, just as He wished *and* saw fit *and* with the best adaptation." (1 Corinthians 12:18 AMP)

We cannot place ourselves where we want to be. We can not choose our assignment. Everyone can't be Pastor, Prophet, Worship Leader, and Sunday School Teacher. You have to be placed and the orders come from God because He has to give you certain equipping to help you in your function.

Self proclaimed titles are worthless. It is not necessary to run around telling people what office you hold. Those who were leaders in the Civil War were known for being honorable and humble men who respected the wishes of those above them and when they rode onto a field, they carried an authority that was noticed by all. A true and appointed leader walks in authority that they themselves do not even realize that they have. The title itself did not instill the confidence of the men but the integrity and attitudes towards the men themselves were what instilled bravery and courage beyond the normal limits. Such qualities, in regards to Stonewall Jackson, caused men within the ranks to say they would charge hell itself for him and a great deal of respect towards him was shown to him from both sides. Even when General Lee rode into the north it was stated that the North wished Lee was their own. Many soldiers during the Civil War stopped to remove their hats when the generals passed by, not because they were told to, but out of honor and respect to those who they recognized were appointed for such a mighty task. It wasn't that these men were not without their own particular quirks or characteristics that at times caused humor or even rebuff, but their leadership abilities caused them to look beyond those things and give respect and honor where respect and honor was due.

So just as every organ, muscle, tendon, joint, and nervous system must function in a human body for it to operate to its fullest capacity, so must the Body of Christ function and operate. For this army to push back and attack and destroy the enemy strongholds we must learn to operate as a team.

These are certainly not all the things that new recruits learn in Boot Camp but they are vital lessons for physical as well as spiritual battle! If these are not learned and implemented in the soldier's life, it will cost him and affect the army over all. Without these basics developed, defeat would be just around the corner. Obedience! Endurance! Procedure! Teamwork!

Chapter 7

Getting Dressed For Battle

Being Clothed in Him

"In conclusion, be strong in the Lord [be empowered through your union with Him]; draw your strength from Him [that strength which His boundless might provides]. Put on God's whole armor [the armor of a heavy-armed soldier which God supplies], that you may be able successfully to stand up against [all] the strategies *and* the deceits of the devil. For we are not wrestling with flesh and blood [contending only with physical opponents], but against the despotisms, against the powers, against [the master spirits who are] the world rulers of this present darkness, against the spirit forces of wickedness in the heavenly (supernatural) sphere. Therefore put on God's complete armor, that you may be able to resist *and* stand your ground on the evil day [of danger], and, having done all [the crisis demands], to stand [firmly in your place]. Stand therefore [hold your ground], having tightened the belt of truth around your loins and having put on the breastplate of integrity *and* of moral rectitude *and* right standing with God, And having shod your feet in preparation [to face the enemy with the firm-footed stability, the promptness, and the readiness produced by the good news] of the Gospel of peace. Lift up over all the [covering] shield of saving faith, upon which you can quench all the flaming missiles of the wicked [one]. And take the helmet of salvation and the sword that the Spirit wields, which is the Word of God. Pray at all times (on every occasion, in every season) in the Spirit, with all [manner of] prayer and entreaty. To that end keep alert and watch with strong purpose *and* perseverance, interceding in behalf of all the saints (God's consecrated people)." (Ephesians 6:10-19 AMP)

"The night is far gone and the day is almost here. Let us then drop (fling away) the works *and* deeds of darkness and put on the [full] armor of light." (Romans 13:12 AMP)

Now that we have gone through Boot Camp and acquired and sharpened our skills we must now dress for battle. No person is ready for battle without the foundation that was laid in Boot Camp. None of our Armed Services takes a recruit, gives him a uniform, slaps a weapon in his hands and places him on the battlefield. This was proven over and over again in the Civil War. There were those who were suddenly given their uniforms and gear but they had never even fired their muskets or learned to maneuver. When the artillery and musket fire rang out, they would drop their weapons and flee out of fear. It wasn't until later in the war when McClellan took over the Army of the Potomac and then organized it and drilled it when it finally became ready for the battle.

So at this point, we are trained and have grown some-what, and now we must dress appropriately. Wearing the right battlefield gear is critical. Battlefield attire is specifi-cally designed for the area or region that the soldiers will be fighting in. One doesn't wear clothing which is better suited to the desert while out in the jungle. The soldier would be an easy target while wearing the wrong camouflage. Also, they would not be adequately equipped for the weather. Proper battle gear for our warfare is essential.

I would like to break down some of the key phrases in the Scripture mentioned above, Ephesians 6:10-19, in order to give some insight into them.

In verse 11 it explains that we are to "put on" the armor. The phrase "put on" comes from the Greek word enduo and means to "envelope in, hide in, be clothed in".

As we all know, God doesn't come down and personally dress us every day. We have to make the effort to be clothed in the armor. The phrase "whole armor" comes from the word panoplia which means "all the weapons; in full armor; a heavily armed soldier; a walking arsenal". This is complete equipment without lacking one single piece.

Knox Translation says "you must wear all the weapons in God's armory." Notice the phrase "that ye" means that it is "us" who do the fighting. The armor is not for a dress parade. It is battle gear!

"Stand against" is a soldiers' phrase that means to "stand your ground and not retreat and it speaks of tenacity and fortitude."

"Wiles," comes from the Greek word "methodeia" which means "cunning arts, craft, deceit, trickery." Strategies would be a good translation of this Greek word. Our enemy has plans against us. He is always plotting against those who are in God's army.

The phrase "take unto you" stems from "analambano," which translates, "to take up in order to use." It's a command given with a tone of sharpness and urgency meaning to be obeyed at once.

The Christian is to take up and put on all the armor of God as a once for all act and keep that armor on during the entire course of their life, not relaxing their vigilance.

"Withstand", translated from the word "anthistemi" means "to stand against, oppose, resist."

"Done", or "katergazomai" means "to accomplish, to perform, carry it to its ultimate conclusion." This speaks of thoroughness; not a halfhearted attempt. We are in the battle to make sure that we have implemented everything we know that the Word says we are to do. We are to follow the instructions to the fullest. This is an area where people often fail when they don't follow everything the Word instructs us to do in the situation. We must remember that God has given instructions for a purpose and not just to inform but for soldiers to implement. How can we expect God to step into the battle when we haven't obeyed Him?

"Stand", from the Greek word "histemi" meaning "abide, continue, hold up" has the implication of steadfastness. Stand your ground, don't give an inch. It is the equivalent of drawing the line in the sand and saying I will not move or give in. Here is where faith is put to the real test. The test is to remain unmoved and unflinching in the assault of the enemy. You have obeyed the Word of God and you know that He is faithful so you dig your heels into the ground and refuse to let the enemy take any ground. This is often the critical point of warfare and so many fail at this point. They begin to waver and fall back instead of standing.

How do we do stand? Is it just the armor alone that helps us to do this? The key is in the proceeding verse.

"In conclusion, be strong in the Lord [be empowered through your union with Him]; draw your strength from Him [that strength which His boundless might provides].

The secret is here my friend. Abiding in Him and receiving from Him everything we need to strengthen us and empower us." (Ephesians 6:10 AMP)

"Be strong," from the word "endunamoo" means "to make strong, endue with strength; to clothe yourself in His strength." God, through the Holy Spirit, is the supplier of the strength! God never called you to fight or stand or win your victory in your own power. This will lead to absolute failure and frustration in our lives if we try to do this by just our own strength, willpower and determination. If we do that we are trying to fight by means that were never intended for us to accomplish our victory with.

"Power", derived from the word "kratos" means "relative or manifested power." "Might" from the word "ischuos" is "power as an endowment."

What the Apostle Paul was saying to us when this was written was that we are to be empowered or endued with God's power and might in our spirits that comes from our intimate and continuous union with Him. Therein we find all of God's might and power available in order to fight and stand. It is abiding in Him, not just visiting but abiding. This cannot be emphasized enough in our life. If you try to fight the battle without being intimately connected with Him you will fail!

"SO YOU, my son, be strong (strengthened inwardly) in the grace (spiritual blessing) that is [to be found only] in Christ Jesus. (2 Timothy 2:1 AMP)

As we look at the different pieces of the armor we need to keep in mind that it is representative of what Jesus is to us. It is not just Jesus available to us but Jesus appropriated for us. He is the source of the armor. God supplies it to us through our being in Jesus.

"But clothe yourself with the Lord Jesus Christ (the Messiah), and make no provision for [indulging] the flesh [put a stop to thinking about the evil cravings of your physical nature] to [gratify its] desires (lusts). (Romans 13:14 AMP)

We are to be clothed in Jesus. We "put on" Christ, again pointing to our union with Him.

"For as many [of you] as were baptized into Christ [into a spiritual union and communion with Christ, the Anointed One, the Messiah] have put on (clothed yourselves with) Christ." (Galatians 3:27 AMP)

As we clothe ourselves with Him we become enclosed in that armor that He provides. This is why we must maintain our union with Him and continue abiding in Him. We cannot afford the peril of stepping out from that union and armor into the line of fire of the enemy. Everything that we need to walk in victory is being provided in relationship with Him.

The Armor

In order to discuss the armor, let's divide it into two groups. The first group explains what was appropriated in our lives when we received Jesus Christ. It is what we have already obtained in Him. These are foundational things that should be already established in our lives.

> Group One: Having girded our loins
> Having put on the breastplate
> Having our feet shod

The second group comes as we grow in Him and learn to appropriate what all He has done and offers to us.

> Group Two: Taking the Shield of Faith
> Taking the Helmet of Salvation
> Taking the Sword of the Spirit

The Individual Pieces of Armor

Girdle of Truth

"Stand therefore, having your loins girt about with truth."
Truth is foundational! It is the centerpiece of the whole armor. This belt or girdle was not for style but for function. It held the armor in place close to the body. Often a soldier

was dressed in a tunic, which he would tuck into the girdle so that his movement would not be impeded. After he had put on the belt, he would begin to add the other pieces. Truth is to be our belt. Encircled and girded by Truth.

"Then said Jesus to those Jews which believed on him, If ye continue in my word, *then* are ye my disciples indeed; And ye shall know the truth, and the truth shall make you free." (John 8:31-33)

"Jesus saith unto him, I am the way, the truth, and the life: no man cometh unto the Father, but by me." (John 14:6-7)

Jesus said my Word is truth! Beloved we must have the truth of God's Word settled in our hearts and minds. There should be no wavering! Being rooted in the truth of His word brings us stability during the battle because we know within our hearts the validity and power of the truth of the Word. We stand knowing that God has bound Himself to the Word and watches over it to make sure that it comes to pass. Knowing the truth of God's Word will keep our faith from wavering. The truth will protect us from error and delusion. If we become and remain grounded in the Word, we will have truth in us to detect and expose the lies of the enemy.

"That we *henceforth* be no more children, tossed to and fro, and carried about with every wind of doctrine, by the sleight of men, *and* cunning craftiness, whereby they lie in wait to deceive; But speaking the truth in love, may grow up into him in all things, which is the head, *even* Christ." (Ephesians 4:14-16)

"Study to shew thyself approved unto God, a workman that needeth not to be ashamed, rightly dividing the word of truth." (2 Timothy 2:15)

"For the time will come when they will not endure sound doctrine; but after their own lusts shall they heap to themselves teachers, having itching ears; And they shall turn away *their* ears from the truth, and shall be turned unto fables." (2 Timothy 4:3-5)

"Now the Spirit speaketh expressly, that in the latter times some shall depart from the faith, giving heed to seducing spirits, and doctrines of devils; Speaking lies in hypocrisy; having their conscience seared with a hot iron." (1 Timothy 4:1-3)

If there were ever a time that we needed to be girded with truth, it is now. As we move closer to the return of the Lord, strong delusion and deception will increase significantly on the earth. How will we recognize error or deception when we hear it? Just as a bank teller learns to recognize counterfeit money by handling the real money constantly and becoming familiar with it, we will recognize error and deception if we are grounded in the truth of the Word and continually use it to shore up our thinking. The truth will guide us and protect us and anchor us.

Jesus also said in His Word that He is the truth. He did not say I am "a" truth. He said I am "the" Truth! We must be anchored and girded with the truth of Who Jesus is, what He accomplished in our redemption and His place is now as King of kings and Lord of lords. He is all that the Word of God says He is. As we clothe ourselves in Him, we clothe ourselves in truth.

There are many so-called religions that will acknowledge Jesus as a good Teacher, or a good Prophet but not that He was the incarnate Son of God. They claim that He is just one way to a higher spiritual enlightenment. The truth is, that any teaching that does not recognize and proclaim Jesus fully as the Word declares He is; as the Son of God, born in the flesh of a virgin, whose Blood was shed on the Cross for our sins; is presenting a lie from the pit of hell.

"I marvel that ye are so soon removed from him that called you into the grace of Christ unto another gospel: Which is not another; but there be some that trouble you, and would pervert the gospel of Christ. But though we, or an angel from heaven, preach any other gospel unto you than that which we have preached unto you, let him be accursed. As we said before, so say I now again, if any *man* preach any other gospel unto you than that ye have received, let him be accursed." (Galatians 1:6-9)

"Neither is there salvation in any other: for there is none other name under heaven given among men, whereby we must be saved." (Acts 4:12-13)

Jesus is truth personified! There are many lies that have been spread into the lives of mankind that state that there are many paths to God. They claim that all the religions are the same and will lead to enlightenment and salvation. These are lies that have damned people to an eternal darkness forever separated from God's love and mercy. The truth is narrow and there is no gray area in truth. People have bought into these seducing lies and doctrines of demons and have lost their very soul. Truth is a necessity and we must be girded with it.

Breastplate of Righteousness

"And having on the breastplate of righteousness."

"Breastplate," from the Greek word "thoraz" meaning "to cover the breast." In ancient times they called this area the viscera or bowels that they considered contained the seat of emotions. The breastplate in other words covered and protected vital organs. Righteousness here is the Greek word "dikaiosyne" meaning justification.

We are to be protected by our righteousness that comes from being in Him and our right standing in Him. It is not found out of our own merits or works. We are in right standing with the Father because we are in Him (relationship with the Son).

"But now the righteousness of God without the law is manifested, being witnessed by the law and the prophets; Even the righteousness of God *which is* by faith of Jesus

Christ unto all and upon all them that believe: for there is no difference: For all have sinned, and come short of the glory of God; Being justified freely by his grace through the redemption that is in Christ Jesus." (Romans 3:21-24)

"For Moses describeth the righteousness which is of the law, That the man which doeth those things shall live by them. But the righteousness which is of faith speaketh on this wise, Say not in thine heart, Who shall ascend into heaven? (that is, to bring Christ down *from above*:) Or, Who shall descend into the deep? (that is, to bring up Christ again from the dead.) But what saith it? The word is nigh thee, *even* in thy mouth, and in thy heart: that is, the word of faith, which we preach; That if thou shalt confess with thy mouth the Lord Jesus, and shalt believe in thine heart that God hath raised him from the dead, thou shalt be saved. For with the heart man believeth unto righteousness; and with the mouth confession is made unto salvation. For the scripture saith, Whosoever believeth on him shall not be ashamed." (Romans 10:5-11)

"But of him are ye in Christ Jesus, who of God is made unto us wisdom, and righteousness, and sanctification, and redemption: That, according as it is written, He that glorieth, let him glory in the Lord." (1 Corinthians 1:30-31)

"For he hath made him *to be* sin for us, who knew no sin; that we might be made the righteousness of God in him." (2 Corinthians 5:21)

"And be found in him, not having mine own righteousness, which is of the law, but that which is through the faith of Christ, the righteousness which is of God by faith:" (Philippians 3:9-10)

"For by grace are ye saved through faith; and that not of yourselves: *it is* the gift of God: Not of works, lest any man should boast. Our being in Christ provides our righteousness. It is not earned on the basis of performance but by our union in Him." (Ephesians 2:8-10)

"Not by works of righteousness which we have done, but according to his mercy he saved us, by the washing of regeneration, and renewing of the Holy Ghost." (Titus 3:5)

If you are born again you are righteous. When I first began to grasp the understanding of this, it honestly took me a while to comprehend it. It seemed too easy because performance seemed to make better sense. There had to be something I needed to do that would make me righteous. Then the truth of it began to get into my spirit that I was already righteous because of Him. It brought such a relief to my heart and freed me from the concept of having to earn it. However, I do believe there is a practicing side of righteousness.

"And whatsoever we ask, we receive of him, because we keep his commandments, and do those things that are pleasing in his sight." (1 John 3:22)

"May you abound in *and* be filled with the fruits of righteousness (of right standing with God and right doing) which come through Jesus Christ (the Anointed One), to the honor and praise of God [that His glory may be both manifested and recognized]. (Philippians 1:11 AMP)

"And put on the new nature (the regenerate self) created in God's image, [Godlike] in true righteousness and holiness. (Ephesians 4:24 AMP)

"But as for you, O man of God, flee from all these things; aim at *and* pursue righteousness (right standing with God and true goodness), godliness (which is the loving fear of God and being Christlike), faith, love, steadfastness (patience), and gentleness of heart." (1 Timothy 6:11 AMP)

"So whoever cleanses himself [from what is ignoble *and* unclean, who separates himself from contact with contaminating and corrupting influences] will [then himself] be a vessel set apart *and* useful for honorable *and* noble purposes, consecrated *and* profitable to the Master, fit *and* ready for any good work. Shun youthful lusts *and* flee from them, and aim at *and* pursue righteousness (all that is virtuous and good, right living, conformity to the will of God in thought, word, and deed); [and aim at and pursue] faith, love, [and] peace (harmony and concord with others) in fellowship with all [Christians], who call upon the Lord out of a pure heart." (2 Timothy 2:21-22 AMP)

"Every Scripture is God-breathed (given by His inspiration) and profitable for instruction, for reproof *and* conviction of sin, for correction of error *and* discipline in obedience, [and] for training in righteousness (in holy living, in conformity to God's will in thought, purpose, and action)" (2 Timothy 3:16-17 AMP)

Our righteousness comes from our union with Him. Righteousness is manifested through our lives as we seek to please Him. There will be fruits of righteousness produced in our lives by the sanctifying work of the Word and the Holy Spirit in our lives. We aren't talking about getting righteous we are talking about the fruit that should be a natural outgrowth of being righteous. It is a work of sanctification in our lives that springs forth from our position of righteousness. Righteousness comes from our union with Him and though we seek to manifest the fruit of it in our lives, it is not something that we earn. We are the Righteous!

The Feet Shod

"And your feet shod with the preparation of the gospel of peace."

"And having shod your feet in preparation [to face the enemy with the firm-footed stability, the promptness, and the readiness produced by the good news] of the gospel of peace." (Ephesians 6:15 AMP)

Have you ever had shoes that did not fit, they looked wonderful but they were too tight and caused your feet to begin to cramp and the blisters begin to... You could not wait to get them off of your feet. Shoes that do not

113

fit properly will hinder your actions. Every sport requires a certain type of footwear. The proper fit and proper traction are critical for the athlete to perform to the best of his or her ability.

Have you gone shopping for new sneakers lately? I remember when there were two styles to choose from, high tops or low tops, and they were only available in black or white. Today, one would have to do some studying in order to purchase the right shoe. Besides the various colors and brands you now have to consider every activity you might do in them. There are decisions to be made such as if one wants a flex heel or air or the special cushioning. What started out to be a simple shopping trip to buy new sneakers, ends up being a mind numbing and expensive purchase. Why do we endure this? For the simple reason if our feet aren't comfortable, we are miserable.

It is critical in battle to have the proper footwear. In the beginning of the Vietnam War they used a regular standard issue leather army boot. However, in the tropical climate of the country, this caused major problems to develop in the soldiers' feet. It became a major concern and one that caused them to have to implement different footwear.

Shoes; it seems like such an insignificant thing. I found it very interesting that the spark for the Battle of Gettysburg in the Civil War was because of shoes. In the South there was a lack of shoe leather and factories and the Confederate Arm, desperately needed them. There were times when a few shiploads of boots would have done more for the Confederate Army than shiploads of guns. The efficiency of the troops would have been increased tremendously had they been able to obtain footwear. General Robert E. Lee, sending a quest to the Quartermaster from Winchester stated that the camp there were 900 without shoes and there was n in the remainder of the Army who were in need. The Confederate Army was actually positioned north of Gettysburg but some news had come that there were shoes in a warehouse there, so part of the infantry headed there on a shoe run. The Union Army had come in from the south and the commander realized the strategic importance of the town because of the roads leading in and out. General Lee had reported to Richmond that 1,000 pairs of shoes were obtained in Fredericktown, 250 pairs in Williamsport, 400 in Hagerstown but that it was still not enough to cover the bare feet. It has been stated the trail of the Confederate Army could be traced by the bloodstains of the feet along the highway. General Lee was not marching on Gettysburg but heading farther north, but then made the adjustment, because in the search for shoes they encountered the Union forces and thereby embarked upon the bloodiest battle of the Civil War; three days of terrible bloodshed.

Being surefooted was important to the Roman soldiers. They were known to drive nails into their sandals to grip the ground better. This helped them to stand and fight. Back when football was played on grass, before the invention of artificial turf, depending on the surface that they were to play on they would sometimes have to exchange the shorter cleats for longer ones in order to play more surefooted. We need to be surefooted!

Having the peace of God gives us a strong advantage to be able to be stable in the battle. I believe there are several aspects to this kind of peace. First, our peace with God!

"Peace I leave with you, my peace I give unto you: not as the world giveth, give I unto you. Let not your heart be troubled, neither let it be afraid." (John 14:27)

"The word which *God* sent unto the children of Israel, preaching peace by Jesus Christ: (he is Lord of all)" (Acts 10:36-37)

"Therefore being justified by faith, we have peace with God through our Lord Jesus Christ." (Romans 5:1)

"For the kingdom of God is not meat and drink; but righteousness, and peace, and joy in the Holy Ghost." (Romans 14:17)

"Grace *be* unto you, and peace, from God our Father, and *from* the Lord Jesus Christ." (1 Corinthians 1:3)

"But now in Christ Jesus ye who sometimes were far off are made nigh by the blood of Christ. For he is our peace, who hath made both one, and hath broken down the middle wall of partition *between us*; Having abolished in his flesh the enmity, *even* the law of commandments *contained* in ordinances; for to make in himself of twain one new man, *so* making peace." (Ephesians 2:13-15)

"Grace *be* unto you, and peace, from God our Father, and *from* the Lord Jesus Christ." (Philippians 1:2)

"Be careful for nothing; but in every thing by prayer and supplication with thanksgiving let your requests be made known unto God. And the peace of God, which passeth all understanding, shall keep your hearts and minds through Christ Jesus." (Philippians 4:6-7)

"And let the peace of God rule in your hearts, to the which also ye are called in one body; and be ye thankful." (Colossians 3:15)

"And the very God of peace sanctify you wholly; and *I pray God* your whole spirit and soul and body be preserved blameless unto the coming of our Lord Jesus Christ." (1 Thessalonians 5:23)

We can be surefooted in battle because we have peace with God. It will give us strength and keep us stable, knowing in our hearts that we have that blessed peace. It should be a great comfort within us knowing that we have peace with God and are in covenant relation with Him. This peace gives us a tranquility of soul knowing that He is mindful of His covenant and us and hasn't left us, but is with us in the battle.

When we repented of our sins and received Jesus as Lord of our lives we entered that place of peace. Knowing that all is well between God and us should remove every twinge of fear from our beings. It is then that we can see that we have peace from God. We know that it is a fruit produced from our union with Him. It is a peace that comes not from circumstances but from His Spirit. He gives it to us! It should be manifest in our life! It causes us to stand when others fall. Peace is such a stabilizing force within us keeping us from being tossed around especially in our emotions.

When my wife and I went on a cruise for our honeymoon we wondered how much we would feel the tossing of the ocean. Would it bother us at all? Then they informed us about the stabilizers that are used on the ship. It was amazing as we sliced through the water how smooth the sailing of the ship was. If you were on deck, you noticed the waves and the up and down movement of the ship. However, in our cabin it was so smooth that the only way you could observe the motion of the ship was to look out the porthole at the horizon and see the movement of the water. This peace that God gives us acts just like those stabilizers. The storms come and at times it seems the battle rages but we have a perfect peace; a peace that keeps us settled in our hearts and minds. Panic and fear do not grip us but an unwavering assurance that God is in control. This peace should stand as a guard or sentry over our hearts and thoughts.

"And let the peace (soul harmony which comes) from Christ rule (act as umpire continually) in your hearts [deciding and settling with finality all questions that arise in your minds, in that peaceful state] to which as [members of Christ's] one body you were also called [to live]. And be thankful (appreciative), [giving praise to God always]." (Colossians 3:15 AMP)

See, learning to let that peace be an umpire will save you time and energy. If suddenly you feel that peace leaving as you contemplate a major decision, it is a signal that it is time to rethink the decision. Let nothing or no one rob you of that peace. Let it guard your emotions and mind, keeping you surefooted.

Taking the Shield of Faith

"Above all, taking the shield of faith, wherewith ye shall be able to quench all the fiery darts of the wicked." The Twentieth Century translation reads; "at every onslaught take up faith for your shield."

"Shield" comes from the Greek word, "thyreos" which is "a large shield." The idea of this shield was that it was able to cover most of the body. It afforded the most protection to the soldier. The Roman soldiers often carried the shield and they were almost full body length and curved. They could stand shoulder to shoulder and it presented to the enemy a wall of resistance.

Our shield is a critical piece of our armor. It is made of a material of strong capability for it is made of faith.

"Faith" or "Pistis" means "firm persuasion, credence, conviction, belief." It is a full acknowledgement of God's revelation, of His fidelity and nature. It is the full recognition of the fact that God is committed to all that He has revealed and declared.

I believe it is important to have a good understanding of the two-fold application of this word in our lives. First of all I believe this speaks of our beliefs concerning God and His covenant and our redemption. It is about our belief in God's Word and His Character. It is our foundation. It also refers to the spiritual force of faith which is not only implanted into us by God, nurtured and strengthened by His Word, but is under-girded by what we firmly believe in; His nature and Character and Word.

Your belief system is the governing factor of your life. Every decision and action you make is a product of its existence. If it is faulty or weak, you will not endure the battle.

A person without a strong belief core is easily manipulated and controlled by outside forces. It is formed in our lives by our thought patterns, our interpretation of experiences, influences, and knowledge and it flows together to form and lay the foundation of our core beliefs.

"But in your hearts set Christ apart as holy [and acknowledge Him] as Lord. Always be ready to give a logical defense to anyone who asks you to account for the hope that is in you, but do it courteously and respectfully." (1 Peter 3:15 AMP)

Peter said be ready to give a reason for what you believe. The Greek word "reason" means "cause or motive." It has with it the idea of being able to give an adequate thoughtful reply to someone who may ask the reason for the hope within you and why you believe what you believe. Though it may appear spiritual to say, 'Because it is faith,' this is not what is implied here neither is it a call to debate. This would be the same as an attorney being able to build his case by the evidence and the law. Could you present the Gospel in a reasonable manner? Could you state what you believe in a thorough manner? These are the reasons it is very important for us to be grounded in biblical doctrine. We should have a firm foundation in the true doctrines of the Word of God. It is not necessary to become a deep theologian or super-scholar; however we should be able to outline clearly the truth of the Gospel. We need to know why the virgin birth was necessary, how to explain that Jesus is the Son of God, why the Blood was necessary for Redemption, and why the necessity of the Resurrection. All of these are fundamental truths that must be firmly understood and embraced in our hearts and spirits. Without them the enemy will use debates, arguments, and seemingly profound insight and logic to move us in our beliefs. Part of our warfare pertains to this very thing.

"For the weapons of our warfare are not physical [weapons of flesh and blood], but they are mighty before God for the overthrow *and* destruction of strongholds, [Inasmuch as we] refute arguments *and* theories *and* reasonings and every proud *and* lofty thing that sets itself up against the [true] knowledge of God; and we lead every thought *and* purpose away captive into the obedience of Christ (the Messiah, the Anointed One)" (2 Corinthians 10:4-5 AMP)

If we are not covered in the shield of our beliefs we can be easy prey for the enemy to confuse. The enemy has always and will continue to try exalt his wisdom above Gods'. He will always attack the veracity of God's Word. Over the years I have heard a lot of debates and theories that honestly were well thought out and presented with much enthusiasm and forethought. If I had not been grounded in my beliefs I could have been moved off the truth. Being grounded also helps us to keep deception at arms length because we then know the solid biblical truths.

Ignorance is not a blessing! Paul was able, not only with the anointing but also with a manner of presenting the truth, to move upon the people of his day. One of the hardest things for me to see today is a believer portrayed in the movies or television as an overzealous, simple-minded person, while it portrays the ungodly as wise men of wisdom and reasoning. I can't help but wonder, 'Could it be our lack of not being able to articulate the truths in an accurate measure that have caused this characterization?' Know what you believe and why you believe it!

The Force of Faith

We must have an understanding of the power of the force of faith. Faith is not a mindset though it will produce a certain mindset. Faith is not a magical wand that we pull out in times of trouble, it is a lifestyle. Faith does not deny the existence of problems it denies the right of the problem to conquer you. There are several spiritual forces that we have access to. I believe that there are three very distinctive ones that will govern our victory in battle and those are love, hope, and faith. These three are vitally important and work in conjunction one with the other. Each of these in themselves are worthy of investigation and much thought and research, however I want to show the interplay before focusing on faith alone.

Love; if you don't walk in love, your faith will not work!

"For in Jesus Christ neither circumcision availeth any thing, nor uncircumcision; but faith which worketh by love." (Galatians 5:6-7)

"For [if we are] in Christ Jesus, neither circumcision nor uncircumcision counts for anything, but only faith activated *and* energized *and* expressed *and* working through love.

Faith is activated, energized, expressed, works through love. So love is critical to the proper functioning of our faith." (Galatians 5:6 AMP)

Hope; it is the mold or blueprint that faith follows. For concrete to do its proper function it is usually poured into forms that have been built to guide its placement and shape. Such is hope to our faith.

"Now faith is the substance of things hoped for, the evidence of things not seen." (Hebrews 11:1-3)

"NOW FAITH is the assurance (the confirmation, the title deed) of the things [we] hope for, being the proof of things [we] do not see *and* the conviction of their reality [faith perceiving as real fact what is not revealed to the senses]. (Hebrews 11:1 AMP)

Hope gives the blueprint and faith is the title deed to that hope. It is the material that is used to bring that hope to reality. We can see then the importance of these two ingredients, love and hope, how when mixed with our faith they cause it to function properly. Why is faith important?

"But without faith *it is* impossible to please *him*: for he that cometh to God must believe that he is, and *that* he is a rewarder of them that diligently seek him." (Hebrews 11:6-7)

The Word says it is impossible to please God without faith. Is faith just a useful tool? No! Faith is a lifestyle!

"For therein is the righteousness of God revealed from faith to faith: as it is written, The just shall live by faith." (Romans 1:17)

"Now the just shall live by faith: but if *any man* draw back, my soul shall have no pleasure in him." (Hebrews 10:38)

There have been a few misunderstandings that have arisen over the last few years regarding faith. The walk of faith is a lifestyle. It is how we govern our lives and the decisions in our lives. It is not a spiritual little wand that we can wave at our problems in order to make them go away. It is not a handy tool to use just when you have to. If we view it that way then we have misunderstood it.

I have heard people make statements such as, 'I tried to walk in faith but it just doesn't seem to work for me.' In all actuality what they are really saying is that they have heard about the laws of faith and the principles of faith, and they tried to work faith like some kind of a formula instead of making it an integral part of their life. They heard someone teach on it and tried to just mimic it and then failed. This is where so many missed it. Everything regarding the Kingdom operates with the principle of faith and yet simply saying it doesn't work. The problem was not the principle of faith but the way that it was not implemented.

I have heard many teachers on the subject of faith. I know people hear the message and get excited and then go and try to live the way that it was explained to them. They heard the principle but have not developed faith in their own lives. Faith is a lifestyle; it is a constant choice that has to become a part of our life in every area of our lives.

Some have so distorted what they heard that it borders on the ludicrous, such as, 'If you have enough faith you won't have problems.' That is not a true statement. Even Jesus reminded us that we were in the world and would have tribulation; but we could be victorious because He had over-come the world. We will have problems, trials, and tests. However, we will never grow to the level of faith where we will never have to face these. The thing to understand is that through faith we will be victorious over it all. Faith was implanted in your spirit at the new birth.

"For I say, through the grace given unto me, to every man that is among you, not to think *of himself* more highly than he ought to think; but to think soberly, according as God hath dealt to every man the measure of faith." (Romans 12:3-4)

The Greek word "measure" here is "metron" which is "a limited portion or degree of."

"Looking unto Jesus the author and finisher of *our* faith; who for the joy that was set before him endured the cross, despising the shame, and is set down at the right hand of the throne of God." (Hebrews 12:2)

Jesus is the source and the consummation of our faith. Our faith finds its start and completion in Him. We all were given faith in the same way that we have all been supplied with the muscle groups in our bodies, it is up to us how we exercise and develop our faith.

How do we increase our faith?

"So then faith *cometh* by hearing, and hearing by the word of God." (Romans 10:17-18)

Faith comes by hearing the Word of God. As we hear the Word preached or taught and during our study time and meditation, the Holy Spirit breathes the Word into our hearts and causes our faith to arise. Faith does not come by trials. In trials and tests, our patience and endurance are built but faith doesn't come. Our faith is applied and then endurance and patience hold it in place against the problem until we have the victory. If trials and tests built our faith we would all be faith giants. Faith is created within us by the Word that we begin to apply in our situations while we are believing in the truth and power of God. The power of faith is incredible.

"Jesus said unto him, if thou canst believe, all things *are* possible to him that believeth."

Notice He said that all things are possible; not just some things or maybe but that it was possible. Does this mean we must have a huge quantity of faith in order to win in warfare?

"Then Jesus answered and said, O faithless and perverse generation, how long shall I be with you? how long shall I suffer you? bring him hither to me. And Jesus rebuked the devil; and he departed out of him: and the child was cured from that very hour. Then came the disciples to Jesus apart, and said, Why could not we cast him out? And Jesus said unto them, Because of your unbelief: for verily I say unto you, If ye have faith as a grain of mustard seed, ye shall say unto this mountain, Remove hence to yonder place; and it shall remove; and nothing shall be impossible unto you. Howbeit this kind goeth not out but by prayer and fasting." (Matthew 17:17-21)

He said if our faith was just the size of a mustard seed it could still move mountains. That is such a powerful thought. So many think they must have a great quantity of faith to win the victory but we learn here that it is not the case. I like to think of it as concentrated faith. You apply your faith to the problem then stand unwavering with your patience and endurance until the victory is manifested.

"For whatsoever is born of God overcometh the world: and this is the victory that overcometh the world, *even* our faith. Who is he that overcometh the world, but he that believeth that Jesus is the Son of God?" (1 John 5:4-5)

Faith will bring victory!

Taking the Helmet of Salvation

"And take the helmet of salvation." This word for helmet means "to encircle the head." What a vital piece of equipment!

Having played football, I can tell you that I'm thankful for having been made to wear one. If you have ever been head slapped or kneed in the head while trying to tackle you'll know exactly what I'm talking about. As a matter of fact, head slaps were done away with in the NFL because of the severity. Concussions have become a major area of concern in recent years. We used to take great care in the fit of our helmet and we knew for it to do its job properly that it had to fit well.

I love to ride motorcycles with my wife and we both have our helmets. We made sure that they were approved by the Department of Transportation and that they met certain standards of safety. Novelty helmets are cute but they do not offer the level of protection that a D.O.T. approved helmet offers. If you can slip in a bathtub or a wet floor and hit the ground and get head injuries, what would asphalt or concrete do at 25 to 70 mph? It disturbs me sometimes to see people ride without proper riding equipment because I realize the danger that they have exposed themselves to. Even in motor-cycling the rule of thumb is that if you drop your helmet, you should consider replacing it because though it may not show any outer damage you could have compromised the safety if the inner shell. Protecting the head is so vitally important.

In warfare it is an absolute must. The enemy always attacks the mind and ones perspective. The battlefield is in the mind! If the enemy can cause us to waver, question, or to think opposite of the Word of God then he will confuse us. He will twist and pervert our perspective. The enemy preys on the mind. We must guard it all cost.

In warfare, it is a proven maxim that one of the points of strategy is to take the high ground. One reason for this is so that the movement of the enemy can be seen. The enemy knows that we can be controlled by our thoughts. While we can't stop him from attacking our mind we don't have to accept the thoughts that he tries to plant there. We control our thought life, not God. We decide to think on what we choose. The thoughts can be in line with the Word of God or they can be contrary to it. It is why we must learn to do as the Word says and take every thought captive.

"We destroy arguments and every lofty opinion raised against the knowledge of God, and take every thought captive to obey Christ." (2 Corinthians 10:5 ESV)

You are a tri- part being. You are a spirit; you will never cease to exist. You have a soul, which has your mind, will and emotions, and you have an outer shell, which is your body.

"And may the God of peace Himself sanctify you through and through [separate you from profane things, make you pure and wholly consecrated to God]; and may your spirit and soul and body be preserved sound *and* complete [and found] blameless at the coming of our Lord Jesus Christ (the Messiah)." (1 Thessalonians 5:23 AMP)

The soulish realm is where the battle takes place. Your mind and emotions are controlled by what it is that you think about and meditate on. The word "meditate" means "to ponder, muse, think on a subject." Your life moves in the direction of your thoughts.

It has been proven in studies that some motorcycle accidents could have been avoided however the riders' eyesight became fixated on an object in front of them and instead of swerving to avoid the object they instead hit it. The rider didn't refocus on an escape route. In our thoughts, we gravitate towards the thing that is in front of us. Our thoughts can hold us in bondage or help to liberate us. Our minds have the ability to know what the Word of God says concerning subjects and yet still choose to think contrary to it. This is why our mind and thought patterns must be trained. Wrong thinking produces wrong results. Every thought affects our lives and it is vital we think properly. We are empowered or held prisoner by our thoughts. They create the atmosphere of your life.

"For as he thinks in his heart, so is he." (Proverbs 23:7 AMP)

This is a spiritual principle that works in our life for either good or bad. This is where we can fail to win the victory. If we begin to think, 'Well, I know the Bible says that but I think...,' then what we are really doing is lifting our own ideas higher than the spiritual principle. We have to retrain our thought life to be one that is based on and follows Scripture.

"Do not be conformed to this world (this age), [fashioned after and adapted to its external, superficial customs], but be transformed (changed) by the [entire] renewal of your mind [by its new ideals and its new attitude], so that you may prove [for yourselves] what is the good and acceptable and perfect will of God, *even* the thing which is good and acceptable and perfect [in His sight for you]." (Romans 12:2 AMP)

"So this I say and solemnly testify in [the name of] the Lord [as in His presence], that you must no longer live as the heathen (the Gentiles) do in their perverseness [in the folly, vanity, and emptiness of their souls and the futility] of their minds. Their moral understanding is darkened *and* their reasoning is beclouded. [They are] alienated (estranged, self-banished) from the life of God [with no share in it; this is] because of the ignorance (the want of knowledge and perception, the willful blindness) that is deep-seated in them, due to their hardness of heart [to the insensitiveness of their moral nature]. In their spiritual apathy they have become callous *and* past feeling *and* reckless and have abandoned themselves [a prey] to unbridled sensuality, eager *and* greedy to indulge in every form of impurity [that their depraved desires may suggest and demand]. But you did not so learn Christ! Assuming that you have really heard Him *and* been taught by Him, as [all] Truth is in Jesus [embodied and personified in Him], Strip yourselves of your former nature [put off and discard your old unrenewed self] which characterized your previous manner of life and becomes corrupt through lusts *and* desires that spring from delusion; And be constantly renewed in the spirit of your mind [having a fresh mental and spiritual attitude], And put on the new nature (the regenerate self) created in God's image, [Godlike] in true righteousness and holiness." (Ephesians 4:17-25 AMP)

After we are born again, we must begin the discipline of having our mind changed by the Word of God. We must begin to train our thought life to focus on the truth of God's Word, letting the principles contained in it to begin to transform our life. If we think opposite of the Word, it costs us. Carnal thinking, which is controlled thinking without the wisdom of God, will bring death.

"THEREFORE, [there is] now no condemnation (no adjudging guilty of wrong) for those who are in Christ Jesus, *who live [and] walk not after the dictates of the flesh, but after the dictates of the Spirit.* For the law of the Spirit of life [which is] in Christ Jesus [the law of our new being] has freed me from the law of sin and of death. For God has done what the Law could not do, [its power] being weakened by the flesh [the entire nature of man without the Holy Spirit]. Sending His own Son in the guise of sinful flesh and as an offering for sin, [God] condemned sin in the flesh [subdued, overcame, deprived it of its power over all who accept that sacrifice]." (Romans 8:1-17 AMP)

The following Scripture is so vitally important.

"So that the righteous *and* just requirement of the Law might be fully met in us who live *and* move not in the ways of the flesh but in the ways of the Spirit [our lives governed not by the standards and according to the dictates of the flesh, but controlled by the Holy Spirit]. For those who are according to the flesh *and* are controlled by its unholy desires set their minds on *and* pursue those things which gratify the flesh, but those who are according to the Spirit *and* are controlled by the desires of the Spirit set their minds on *and* seek those things which gratify the [Holy] Spirit. Now the mind of the flesh [which is sense and reason without the Holy Spirit] is death [death that comprises all the miseries arising from sin, both here and hereafter]. But the mind of the [Holy] Spirit is life and [soul] peace [both now and forever]. [That is] because the mind of the flesh [with its carnal thoughts and purposes] is hostile to God, for it does not submit itself to God's Law; indeed it cannot. So then those who are living the life of the flesh [catering to the appetites and impulses of their carnal nature] cannot please *or* satisfy God, *or* be acceptable to Him. But you are not living the life of the flesh, you are living the life of the Spirit, if the [Holy] Spirit of God [really] dwells within you [directs and controls you]. But if anyone does not possess the [Holy] Spirit of Christ, he is none of His [he does not belong to Christ, is not truly a child of God]. But if Christ lives in you, [then although] your [natural] body is dead by reason of sin *and* guilt, the spirit is alive because of [the] righteousness [that He imputes to you]. And if the Spirit of Him Who raised up Jesus from the dead dwells in you, [then] He Who raised up Christ *Jesus* from the dead will also restore to life your mortal (short-lived, perishable) bodies through His Spirit Who dwells in you. So then, brethren, we are debtors, but not to the flesh [we are not obligated to our carnal nature], to live [a life ruled by the standards set up by the dictates] of the flesh. For if you live according to [the dictates of] the flesh, you will surely die. But if through the power of the [Holy] Spirit you are [habitually] putting to death (making extinct, deadening) the [evil] deeds prompted by the body, you shall [really and genuinely] live forever. For all who are led by the Spirit of God are sons of God. For [the Spirit which] you have now received [is] not a spirit of slavery to put you once more in bondage to fear, but you have received the Spirit of adoption [the Spirit producing sonship] in [the bliss of] which we cry, Abba (Father)! Father! The Spirit Himself [thus] testifies together with our own spirit, [assuring us] that we are children of God. And if we are [His] children, then we are [His] heirs also: heirs of God and fellow heirs with Christ [sharing His inheritance with Him]; only we must share His suffering if we are to share His glory." (Romans 8 :1-17 AMP)

Carnal thinking cannot understand Spiritual truth. Truth has to be revealed to us by the Spirit of God. A person may read, but though they understand the words, it is possible that they still do not comprehend the truth of it. A Christian can be a child of God but still think carnally which causes them to walk contrary to God's principles and leaves a door for the enemy to attack.

"HOWEVER, BRETHREN, I could not talk to you as to spiritual [men], but as to nonspiritual [men of the flesh, in whom the carnal nature predominates], as to mere infants [in the new life] in Christ [unable to talk yet!] I fed you with milk, not solid food, for you were not yet strong enough [to be ready for it]; but even yet you are not strong enough [to be ready for it], For you are still [unspiritual, having the nature] of the flesh [under the control of ordinary impulses]. For as long as [there are] envying and jealousy *and* wrangling and factions among you, are you not unspiritual *and* of the flesh, behaving yourselves after a human standard *and* like mere (unchanged) men?" (1 Corinthians 3:1-3 AMP)

Paul was writing to the Believers at Corinth. They were still acting carnal. If we don't let the Word of God and the Holy Spirit work in our life we will never be the warrior God intended for us to be.

"For even though by this time you ought to be teaching others, you actually need someone to teach you over again the very first principles of God's Word. You have come to need milk, not solid food. For everyone who continues to feed on milk is obviously inexperienced *and* unskilled in the doctrine of righteousness (of conformity to the divine will in purpose, thought, and action), for he is a mere infant [not able to talk yet]! But solid food is for full-grown men, for those whose senses *and* mental faculties are trained by practice to discriminate *and* distinguish between what is morally good *and* noble and what is evil *and* contrary either to divine or human law." (Hebrews 5:12-14 AMP)

Notice here he says they trained by practice. A truly mature believer has done this. They have allowed the Word and the Spirit to change them. A person will always live in defeat if they continue to walk with a carnal mind. The Holy Spirit's main job is to reveal the truths of the Word of God. God has not left us helpless in understanding His Word. Read the following passage slowly and prayerfully.

"And my language and my message were not set forth in persuasive (enticing and plausible) words of wisdom, but they were in demonstration of the [Holy] Spirit and power [a proof by the Spirit and power of God, operating on me and stirring in the minds of my hearers the most holy emotions and thus persuading them], So that your faith might not rest in the wisdom of men (human philosophy), but in the power of God. Yet when we are among the full-grown (spiritually mature Christians who are ripe in understanding), we do impart a [higher] wisdom (the knowledge of the divine plan previously hidden); but it is indeed not a wisdom of this present age *or* of this world nor of the leaders *and* rulers of this age, who are being brought to nothing *and* are doomed to pass away. But rather what we are setting forth is a wisdom of God once hidden [from the human understanding] and now revealed to us by God—[that wisdom] which God devised *and* decreed before the ages for our glorification [to lift us into the glory of His presence]. None of the rulers of this age *or* world perceived *and* recognized *and* understood this, for if they had, they would never have crucified the Lord of glory. But, on the contrary, as the Scripture says, What eye has not seen and ear has not heard and has not entered into the heart of man, [all that] God has prepared (made and keeps ready) for those who love Him [who hold

Him in affectionate reverence, promptly obeying Him and gratefully recognizing the benefits He has bestowed]. Yet to us God has unveiled *and* revealed them by *and* through His Spirit, for the [Holy] Spirit searches diligently, exploring *and* examining everything, even sounding the profound and bottomless things of God [the divine counsels and things hidden and beyond man's scrutiny]. For what person perceives (knows and understands) what passes through a man's thoughts except the man's own spirit within him? Just so no one discerns (comes to know and comprehend) the thoughts of God except the Spirit of God. Now we have not received the spirit [that belongs to] the world, but the [Holy] Spirit Who is from God, [given to us] that we might realize *and* comprehend *and* appreciate the gifts [of divine favor and blessing so freely and lavishly] bestowed on us by God. And we are setting these truths forth in words not taught by human wisdom but taught by the [Holy] Spirit, combining *and* interpreting spiritual truths with spiritual language [to those who possess the Holy Spirit]. But the natural, non-spiritual man does not accept *or* welcome *or* admit into his heart the gifts *and* teachings *and* revelations of the Spirit of God, for they are folly (meaningless nonsense) to him; and he is incapable of knowing them [of progressively recognizing, understanding, and becoming better acquainted with them] because they are spiritually discerned *and* estimated *and* appreciated. But the spiritual man tries all things [he examines, investigates, inquires into, questions, and discerns all things], yet is himself to be put on trial and judged by no one [he can read the meaning of everything, but no one can properly discern *or* appraise *or* get an insight into him]. For who has known *or* understood the mind (the counsels and purposes) of the Lord so as to guide *and* instruct Him *and* give Him knowledge? But we have the mind of Christ (the Messiah) *and* do hold the thoughts (feelings and purposes) of His heart." (1 Corinthians 2:4-16 AMP)

Our thought life must be trained and guarded. Meditating the Word of God is critical and needs to be implemented in a greater way in the Body of Christ.

To have the armor in the first place we must be saved. The Helmet of Salvation: the word for salvation can be translated "safety or salvation." What does the word Salvation mean to you? Does it mean you are born again, your sins forgiven and eventually you will make heaven? While that certainly is an important part, it is too narrow in its scope. The Greek word for "salvation" or "sozo" does include all of that definition but it also includes all the blessings bestowed by God on those who are in Christ. It means wholeness. It encompasses everything about your life spiritually, physically, and emotionally, or your soulish area which includes your mind, will and emotions. What a powerful thing! God wants us whole and nothing was left out of our redemption. So when we get into the Word of God and learn our salvation is all encompassing, we also learn that it includes encircling our thoughts to guard and protect us against the assault of the enemy.

"For the weapons of our warfare are not physical [weapons of flesh and blood], but they are mighty before God for the overthrow *and* destruction of strongholds, [Inasmuch as we] refute arguments *and* theories *and* reasonings and every proud *and* lofty thing that sets itself up against the [true] knowledge of God; and we lead every thought *and* purpose away captive into the obedience of Christ (the Messiah, the Anointed One). (2 Corinthians 10:4-5 AMP)

"BLESSED (HAPPY, fortunate, prosperous, and enviable) is the man who walks *and* lives not in the counsel of the ungodly [following their advice, their plans and purposes], nor stands [submissive and inactive] in the path where sinners walk, nor sits down [to relax and rest] where the scornful [and the mockers] gather. But his delight *and* desire are in the law of the Lord, and on His law (the precepts, the instructions, the teachings of God) he habitually meditates (ponders and studies) by day and by night." (Psalms 1:1-2 AMP)

"Let the words of my mouth and the meditation of my heart be acceptable in Your sight, O Lord, my [firm, impenetrable] Rock and my Redeemer." (Psalms 19:14 AMP) "May my meditation be sweet to Him; as for me, I will rejoice in the Lord." (Psalms 104:34 AMP)

"Oh, how love I Your law! It is my meditation all the day. You, through Your commandments, make me wiser than my enemies, for [Your words] are ever before me. I have better understanding *and* deeper insight than all my teachers, because Your testimonies are my meditation. I understand more than the aged, because I keep Your precepts [hearing, receiving, loving, and obeying them]." (Psalms 119:97-100 AMP)

"My eyes anticipate the night watches *and* I am awake before the cry of the watchman, that I may meditate on Your word." (Psalms 119:148 AMP)

The Sword of the Spirit

"And the sword of the Spirit, which is the word of God."

"And take the helmet of salvation and the sword that the Spirit wields, which is the Word of God." (Ephesians 6:17 AMP)

Notice that it is the Spirit that wields or operates the Sword! This is not an insignificant thing. In fact, it is critical to understanding the power of the Sword. God has put value on His Word. This is one reason that the Word is a mighty weapon.

"Forever, O Lord, Your word is settled in heaven [stands firm as the heavens]." (Psalms 119:89 AMP)

"My covenant will I not break *or* profane, nor alter the thing that is gone out of My lips." (Psalms 89:34-35 AMP)

"Then said the Lord to me, You have seen well, for I am alert *and* active, watching over My word to perform it." (Jeremiah 1:12 AMP)

" For as the rain and snow come down from the heavens, and return not there again, but water the earth and make it bring forth and sprout, that it may give seed to the sower and bread to the eater, So shall My word be that goes forth out of My mouth: it shall not return to Me void [without producing any effect, useless], but it shall accomplish that which I please *and* purpose, and it shall prosper in the thing for which I sent it." (Isaiah 55:10-11 AMP)

"[A Psalm] of David. I WILL confess *and* praise You [O God] with my whole heart; before the gods will I sing praises to You. I will worship toward Your holy temple and praise Your name for Your loving-kindness and for Your truth *and* faithfulness; for You have exalted above all else Your name and Your word *and* You have magnified Your word above all Your name!" (Psalms 138:1-2 AMP)

"And the Lord utters His voice before His army, for His host is very great, and [they are] strong *and* powerful who execute [God's] word. For the day of the Lord is great and very terrible, and who can endure it?" (Joel 2:11 AMP)

We can see by these Scriptures the high premium that God has put on His Word. All of heaven stands ready to back the Word of God. All of the resources of heaven are placed behind the Word. Notice God watches over it, He will not allow it to return to Him without it producing the results that He has spoken. This makes me want to shout! When God has spoken forth something we can be assured it shall come to pass without fail. Everything God is stands behind every utterance He speaks!

"God is not a man, that He should tell *or* act a lie, neither the son of man, that He should feel repentance *or* compunction [for what He has promised]. Has He said and shall He not do it? Or has He spoken and shall He not make it good?" (Numbers 23:19 AMP)

We can have confidence in His Word. "Logos" is the written Word of God. It is the Word that was written down by men as they heard and obeyed the Spirit of God. There is no way to list all the Scriptures that refer to the written Word of God. Even Jesus in quoting the Prophets would say, "It is written..."

I am so thankful for the written Word of God. I love to read and meditate on it, to see all the truths contained within and the promises that are so freely given to us. Reading the Word (Logos) is very important in our walk with the Lord. We must understand that they are not just words printed on paper; but that it is full of power and life.

"For the Word that God speaks is alive and full of power [making it active, operative, energizing, and effective]; it is sharper than any two-edged sword, penetrating to the dividing line of the breath of life (soul) and [the immortal] spirit, and of joints and marrow [of the deepest parts of our nature], exposing *and* sifting *and* analyzing *and* judging the very thoughts and purposes of the heart." (Hebrews 4:12 AMP)

The Word is alive, operative, and energizing!

"Rhema" is a logos word that has been breathed upon and made alive in our spirits and has been energized to our spirits in a profound way. It was breathed upon by the Holy Spirit to us so that a confidence and faith arises as never before. We no longer just read it and agree with it but all of a sudden it becomes alive and is burned into our spirit that we can stand unmoving upon it.

Many years ago, I was facing a great attack of the enemy. It was an attack that had the possibility of ruining my life and my reputation. I felt as though my back was against the wall. I went to my knees seeking to hear from the Lord. In wondering what I was to do and while trying to sort through the advice that others were trying to offer to me, I knew only to seek the Lord with tenacity and tears. As I was praying, I suddenly heard the voice of the Lord say this simple phrase, "Cast not away your confidence." This kept ringing in my heart and ears and was never forgotten during this time of attack. I held on to that phrase to get me through the battle. Each time that I would pray concerning this, the Holy Spirit would reaffirm those words to me. I found it written!

"Cast not away therefore your confidence, which hath great recompence of reward." (Hebrews 10:35)

This is all I got; the only thing it seemed the Lord would speak to me. Honestly, during that time I was hoping for some great impartation of knowledge and direction and instead I heard this sentence over and over again. Yet, the Holy Spirit breathed it into my spirit and an unshakeable faith arose within me while a peace that surpassed all understanding began to settle in my spirit. Every time the enemy would try to attack my mind and each time my thoughts would start to waver, I would think on what the Holy Spirit had said to me. I still had to walk through the trial, but I walked not in fear but with a confidence that God was in control. God Himself represented me and by the time this attack was over, I was vindicated!

In 1995, in Birmingham, Alabama, I was preaching at a Wednesday evening service on "The Power of Our Covenant." Suddenly during the message, Scripture after Scripture began to roll out of my mouth concerning angels and God protecting and delivering us. I wondered why the Spirit of God was moving me in this direction because I didn't study this for the message and it certainly was not in my notes. I had learned to just flow in the Spirit while preaching and every time this would happen, these Scriptures seemed to explode within me!

After the service I went to my car and while starting it up and putting the car in reverse, I was approached by a young man. My first thought was that he must have a question for

me regarding the message I had delivered, however, I immediately sensed in my spirit that I was not to completely roll
the window down. Suddenly, this unknown assailant lifted a
gun and while I started backing the car away, he shot me in
the face, through the driver side window.

The enemy had tried to end my life that night and God
knew that this attack was coming. The Holy Spirit moved
me to declare boldly the Word of God, the very Word that
was needed for my upcoming circumstance, and my spirit-
man was being built up to walk through the battle. At that
point I knew that the Word of God and listening to the voice
and direction of the Holy Spirit was what guided me through
this attack. It was the very armor of God, and my realization
of it, that protected me.

The bullet lodged in my face but did not shatter bone or
damage the nerves. While at the time it looked much worse
than it was, today all that is left is a little scar and the bullet
fragments that they removed.

God is so good! I am convinced as that anointed Word
began to roll out of my mouth it stopped the plan of the
enemy to take my life.

Notice the phrase again, "the sword which the Spirit
wields." This is vital for us to understand. While in the
battle, we can recall to mind the logos (written word), that
is given in the Word of God, however mental assent is not
enough. Every battle we face will have a key to unlock the
victory. This is why we must go to the Father and get His
instructions.

Recently, God began to unveil more to me about
speaking His Word and confessing His Word. Many have
misunderstood this teaching and began to apply it inaccu-
rately in their lives. There are many who began to belittle
this teaching, scorn it and even ridicule it. One can't obtain
Salvation without confessing. What we speak is important!
Words are important! Don't get rid of a principle because

some have misunderstood it. The logos or written Word was never meant to be spoken in vain repetitions as though it were some magical incantation or formula that would produce what we wanted. We are to take the written Word and meditate on it, put our trust in that promise or command and then allow the Holy Spirit of God to breathe upon it and energize it to us. Then, it is not just a mental affirmation that we agree with but it becomes an unshakeable faith in our spirit because it has been energized or made rhema to us. Though it may be a whole verse or just a phrase, it will come out of your spirit and then your mouth and will work mightily against the very thing that you are fighting.

When this is learned, walked out and applied, you will stand in the face of hell unmoved in your faith. This is the difference! We are not to run around just quoting verses but faith-filled energized, quickened words anointed of the Holy Spirit!

"Who is he who speaks and it comes to pass, if the Lord has not authorized *and* commanded it?" (Lamentations 3:37 AMP)

Allow the Holy Spirit to energize His Words of truth to you and make it alive in your spirit. I love the logos and yes I stand on the promises of God. It is the Word of God that drives me! I love the Word but I know that it is when I come from the presence of the Father and He by the Spirit, takes what He has spoken and makes it come alive to me, with an unshakeable faith, that I then come declaring, "Thus saith the Lord!" It is then that it is mixed with faith and the power to bring it to pass. It is the anointed words coming out of your mouth that penetrates the enemy and causes him to retreat. Let the Holy Spirit wield the Sword through your mouth as a mighty weapon against the power of the enemy.

The Armor of God is a powerful tool given to us to withstand the assaults of the enemy and to move forward in victory. Notice the phrase from the Scripture above where it says "the Armor of Light." The word "light" means "to shine, make manifest especially by rays, such as rays of light." I believe those rays are part of the Glory of God that is to be in our life and that shines forth to others. The armor is part of His Glory!

Chapter 8

Warfare Weaponry

Now that we have been properly suited for the battle we must now become acquainted with some of the weapons in our arsenal. These weapons have no defense. There is nothing the enemy has that is more powerful than the weapons that we have spiritually been given access to. As a matter of fact, in the spirit realm, our weapons could be likened to the atomic or nuclear level while in comparison imagine the enemy still uses muskets and slingshots. The enemy can not invent new weapons and God has no need to invent new ones because what He has supplied is more than sufficient. If we learn to handle these weapons accurately we will walk in victory. We must realize God formed these weapons. He designed their purpose and their potency for He knew what it would take to defeat the enemy.

"For though we walk in the flesh, we do not war after the flesh; (For the weapons of our warfare *are* not carnal, but mighty through God to the pulling down of strong holds.)" (2 Corinthians 10:3-4)

"For though we walk (live) in the flesh, we are not carrying on our warfare according to the flesh *and* using mere human weapons. For the weapons of our warfare are not physical [weapons of flesh and blood], but they are mighty before God for the overthrow *and* destruction of strongholds" (2 Corinthians 10:3-4 AMP)

We are not left to fight this battle with our own power, strength and knowledge. The source of the weaponry is not from the mind or plans of men but fashioned by the hand of God. Notice it says they are mighty through God. It is through our union with Him that these weapons are employed for us to implement them for destruction of the strongholds of the enemy. The enemy we fight is in the spirit realm and in this realm the weapons God has forged are powerful, accurate, and deadly to the enemy.

The Arsenal

The Blood

From the beginning blood was God's provision for life both in the natural and in the spiritual. Life is in the blood, or carries life. (Lev. 17:11). From the moment of man's fall God's answer was blood. (Gen. 3:21) The animals were slain as a sacrifice to cover the sins of Adam and Eve. All through the Old Testament the sacrifices were required to atone or cover man's sin. It wasn't the meat that was important, but it was the blood. All the sacrifices offered in the Old Testament were a type or shadow of that ultimate sacrifice that Jesus would make.

Though there are many offerings under the Law, I want to focus on the Sin Offering for Atonement. (Lev. Ch. 16) The Hebrew word "atonement" means "to cover, cleanse, purge, and make reconciliation." I look at this as to mean "to make at one with God." Man was estranged with God because of sin and God who is Holy, was estranged from man because of the necessity to judge sin.

In the Old Testament, the Mercy Seat was located in the Tabernacle between the Cherubim and on top of the Ark of the Covenant where the presence of God dwelt. Once a year, God required that the blood of the bullock and goat be sprinkled upon the Mercy Seat. God's instructions were that only the high priest could enter the Holy of Holies and that the blood was to be sprinkled on the eastward side of the Mercy Seat. (I find it an interesting observation that when God made Adam leave the Garden of Eden, they were sent out of the eastern side and it was there that He placed the Cherubim with flaming swords to guard it from reentry.)

When the High Priest entered to do these things that God required, a rope was attached to him in case the offering was not accepted and he was judged by death. In this case, the dead priest would be pulled out by the rope so that others would not have to enter to remove him. The blood was sprinkled before the Mercy Seat by the High Priest, who was required to do this seven times, signifying completion. Then the High Priest went and applied the blood to the Altar. Before the blood was applied to man God accepted it. Then the High Priest laid his hands upon the other goat and imputed the sins of the people onto the goat, which was sent off into the wilderness bearing the iniquity. Then the Glory of God came forth in the Holy of Holies. What a beautiful picture of what was accomplished in Jesus' death on the cross and the presence and Glory of God that then became accessible to us all when the veil was rent in two!

In the Old Testament, when God looked down on the Ark, which contained a copy of the Law given to Moses, He saw the Mercy Seat located above it. God could see where the Law demanded judgment. However, in looking at the Law, He had to see through the blood, which cried mercy and represented atonement over the judgment of the Law. That is such a powerful thought. When we relate that today to the ultimate sacrifice that Jesus gave at the Cross, it is easy to shout, "Thank God for the Blood!"

Our own approach today to God is by the blood. (Heb. 10:20-22) and this all points us to the price of Calvary. The only thing to redeem man was the blood. So now we see the animals that were used had to be pure and without blemish. This points us to the fact of Jesus' virgin birth because He was without sin; born out from under the dominion of sin and we know that the blood of the father flows though the child. Mary being overshadowed and made pregnant by the Holy Spirit shows that the blood that flowed through Jesus was divine. Oh the power of this! Now we can understand what Paul wrote.

"NOW EVEN the first covenant had its own rules *and* regulations for divine worship, and it division *or* compartment of which were the lampstand and the table with [its loaves of] the showbread set forth. [This portion] is called the Holy Place. But [inside] beyond the second curtain *or* veil, [there stood another] tabernacle [division] known as the Holy of Holies. It had the golden altar of incense and the ark (chest) of the covenant, covered over with wrought gold. This [ark] contained a golden jar, which held the manna and the rod of Aaron that sprouted and the [two stone] slabs of the covenant [bearing the Ten Commandments]. Above [the ark] and overshadowing the mercy seat were the representations of the cherubim [winged creatures which were the symbols] of glory. We cannot now go into detail about these things. These arrangements having thus been made, the priests enter [habitually] into the outer division of the tabernacle in performance of their ritual acts of worship. But into the second [division of the tabernacle] none but the high priest goes, and he only once a year, and never without taking a sacrifice of blood with him, which he offers for himself and for the errors *and* sins of ignorance *and* thoughtlessness which the people have committed. By this the Holy Spirit points out that the way into the [true Holy of] Holies is not yet thrown open as long as the former [the outer portion of the] tabernacle remains a recognized institution *and* is still standing, Seeing that that first [outer portion of the] tabernacle was a parable (a visible symbol or type or picture of the present age). In it gifts and sacrifices are offered, and yet are incapable of perfecting the conscience *or* of cleansing *and* renewing the inner man of the worshiper. For [the ceremonies] deal only with clean and unclean meats and drinks and different washings, [mere] external rules *and* regulations for the body imposed to tide the worshipers over until the time of setting things straight [of reformation, of the complete new order when Christ, the Messiah, shall establish the reality of what these things foreshadow—a better covenant]. But [that appointed time came] when Christ (the Messiah) appeared as a High Priest of the better things that have come *and* are to come. [Then] through the greater and more perfect tabernacle not made with [human] hands, that is, not a part of this material creation, He went once for all into the [Holy of] Holies [of heaven], not by virtue of the blood of goats and calves [by which to make reconciliation between God and man], but His own blood, having found *and* secured a complete redemption (an everlasting release for us). For if [the mere] sprinkling of unholy *and* defiled persons with blood of goats and bulls and with the ashes of a burnt heifer is sufficient for the purification of the body, How much more surely shall the blood of Christ, Who by virtue of [His] eternal Spirit [His own preexistent divine personality] has offered Himself as an unblemished sacrifice to God, purify our consciences from dead works *and* lifeless observances to serve the [ever] living God? [Christ, the Messiah] is therefore the Negotiator *and* Mediator of an [entirely] new agreement (testament, covenant), so that those who are called *and* offered it may receive the fulfillment of the promised everlasting inheritance—since a death has taken place which rescues *and* delivers *and* redeems them from the transgressions committed under the [old] first agreement. For where there is a [last] will *and* testament involved, the death of the one who made it must be established, For a will *and* testament is valid and takes effect only at death, since it has no force *or* legal power as long as the one who made it is alive. So even the [old] first covenant (God's will) was not inaugurated *and* ratified *and* put in force without the shedding of blood. For when every command of the Law had been read out by Moses to all the people, he took the blood of slain calves and goats, together with water and scarlet wool and with a bunch of hyssop, and sprinkled both the Book (the roll of the Law and covenant) itself and all the people, Saying these words: This is the blood that seals *and* ratifies the agreement (the testament, the covenant) which God commanded [me to deliver to] you. And in the same way he sprinkled with the blood both the tabernacle and all the [sacred] vessels *and* appliances used in [divine] worship. [In fact] under the Law almost everything is purified by means of blood, and without the shedding of blood there is neither release from sin *and* its guilt *nor* the remission of the due *and* merited punishment for sins. By such means, therefore, it was necessary for the [earthly] copies of the heavenly things to be purified, but the actual heavenly things themselves [required far] better *and* nobler sacrifices than these. For Christ (the Messiah) has not entered into a sanctuary made with [human] hands, only a copy *and* pattern *and* type of the true one, but [He has entered] into heaven itself, now to appear in the [very] presence of God on our behalf. Nor did He [enter into the heavenly sanctuary to] offer Himself regularly again and again, as the high priest enters the [Holy of] Holies every year with blood not his own. For then would He often have had to suffer [over and over again] since the foundation of the world. But as it now is, He has once for all at the consummation *and* close of the ages appeared to put away *and* abolish sin by His sacrifice [of Himself]. And just as it is appointed for [all] men once to die, and after that the [certain] judgment, Even so it is that Christ, having been offered to take upon Himself *and* bear as a burden the sins of many once *and* once for all, will appear a second time, not to carry any burden of sin *nor* to deal with sin, but to bring to full salvation those who are [eagerly, constantly, and patiently] waiting for *and* expecting Him." (Hebrews 9:1-28 AMP)

"FOR SINCE the Law has merely a rude outline (foreshadowing) of the good things to come—instead of fully expressing those things—it can never by offering the same sacrifices continually year after year make perfect those who approach [its altars]. For if it were otherwise, would [these sacrifices] not have stopped being offered? Since the worshipers had once for all been cleansed, they would no longer have any guilt *or* consciousness of sin. But [as it is] these sacrifices annually bring a fresh remembrance of sins [to be atoned for], Because the blood of bulls and goats is powerless to take sins away. Hence, when He [Christ] entered into the world, He said, Sacrifices and offerings You have not desired, but instead You have made ready a body for Me [to offer]; In burnt offerings and sin offerings You have taken no delight. Then I said, Behold, here I am, coming to do Your will, O God—[to fulfill] what is written of Me in the volume of the Book. When He said just before, You have neither desired, nor have You taken delight in sacrifices and offerings and burnt offerings and sin offerings—all of which are offered according to the Law— He then went on to say, Behold, [here] I am, coming to do Your will. Thus He does away with *and* annuls the first (former) order [as a means of expiating sin] so that He might inaugurate *and* establish the second (latter) order. And in accordance with this will [of God], we have been made holy (consecrated and sanctified) through the offering made once for all of the body of Jesus Christ (the Anointed One). Furthermore, every [human] priest stands [at his altar of service] ministering daily, offering the same sacrifices over and over again, which never are able to strip [from every side of us] the sins [that envelop us] *and* take them away—Whereas this One [Christ], after He had offered a single sacrifice for our sins [that shall avail] for all time, sat down at the right hand of God, then to wait until His enemies should be made a stool beneath His feet. For by a single offering He has forever completely cleansed *and* perfected those who are consecrated *and* made holy. And also the Holy Spirit adds His testimony to us [in confirmation of this]. For having said, This is the agreement (testament, covenant) that I will set up *and* conclude with them after those days, says the Lord: I will imprint My laws upon their hearts, and I will inscribe them on their minds (on their inmost thoughts and understanding.)" (Hebrews 10:1-16 AMP)

The importance of this is to understand the awesome power that is in the Blood of Jesus that makes it such a powerful weapon! The enemy has to honor that Blood, what it stands for and what it represents! He has no defense for the Blood. When we as believers stand upon the efficiency of that Blood, realizing what it means to us, it stops the enemy.

In the early days you would often hear people say in their prayer time, "I plead the Blood!" It is not the repetitive saying of the words that was effective but it is invoking or declaring what the Blood has paid for in our Redemption. By the words of our mouth we declare what the Blood has accomplished and redeemed us from. It is important to study further and to learn how to declare and speak forth the power that the Blood of Jesus contains.

This is why our Covenant is so powerful. If the Old Covenant, which contained the blood of bulls and goats, yet was incomplete as far as dealing with the problem of sin was such a powerful thing, how much more powerful then is our Covenant today which is sealed with the holy eternal blood of the Lord Jesus! If the Abrahamic Covenant contained mighty promises of healing, deliverance, and provision could our Covenant be any less powerful? NO! (Heb. 8:6-13). This

Covenant today was not made between God and man as the Abrahamic Covenant was. Our Covenant was made between the Father and the Son. (Gal. 3:13-18). The eternal, divine Blood of God's own Son, is what sealed this Covenant. This Blood did not cover the sin of man but blotted it out; erased it! (Col. 2:13-15) Oh the Blood of Jesus; that crimson thread that runs through the entire Word of God! What a magnificent truth!

"And they overcame him by the blood of the Lamb, and by the word of their testimony; and they loved not their lives unto the death." (Revelation 12:11)

Oh beloved declare the Blood. The enemy is fully aware of its power! Apply it to every aspect of your life, including your loved ones, your health, your finances, and your home. Shout it – "I am Blood bought!"

The Name of Jesus!

The majesty in the name of Jesus! The very mention of that name causes the hordes of hell to tremble. Even the demons recognize that name. (Acts 19) All of heaven stands behind that name.

"And there is salvation in *and* through no one else, for there is no other name under heaven given among men by *and* in which we must be saved." (Acts 4:12 AMP)

"Wherefore God also hath highly exalted him, and given him a name which is above every name: That at the name of Jesus every knee should bow, of *things* in heaven, and *things* in earth, and *things* under the earth; And *that* every tongue should confess that Jesus Christ *is* Lord, to the glory of God the Father. (Philippians 2:9-11)

"Being made so much better than the angels, as he hath by inheritance obtained a more excellent name than they." (Hebrews 1:4)

In Acts Chapter 4, one of my favorite passages in the Bible deals with the power of the name of Jesus, Peter is being asked, "By what power or authority do you heal this man?" Peter responds to say that it is not because I am an Apostle, or that I have in myself some great power but by the name of Jesus and faith in that name. All that Jesus is has been placed in that name! Grasp the significance of that! The Redeemer, the Anointed One, the High Priest, the Mediator, the King of kings, the Great Physician, the Way, the Truth and the Light! All of this and so much more is encapsulated in that name. When we speak the name of Jesus, all the earthly and spiritual realm knows and recognizes the authority and the exaltedness of that name.

You see, when we use our Covenant right to speak the name of Jesus, it is His authority behind the order or the decree. We come by order of the King and just as an Ambassador who represents the government has the right to say, "I speak on behalf of the government" we have the right to use the name of Jesus and in everything He is recognized. Oh, may be it granted to us the ability to see the power of that name and the honor and glory that has been divinely assigned to that name. May we fully comprehend all that God invested in that precious name.

"In Jesus Name," means to act in His stead while fully authorized to use the authority associated with it. We have, through relationship with Him, obtained position of legal standing, just as an attorney would speak on our behalf, we may speak on His behalf. We were born into the family of God, baptized in that name, then the name that was conferred upon Jesus was then given to us, by Jesus, to use as His representatives in order to continue His ministry in the earth with His anointing and to demolish the strongholds of the enemy. What a privilege! We do not use the name as some kind of incantation but we wield it as a weapon against the enemy who must submit to His authority.

Jesus told us to pray with the addendum of "My name." (John 14: 12-13, 16:23-24). Jesus did not say for His names sake. He is not the one in need or with the petition. We use the name to once again come from the standing of Covenant to obtain what is needed. I am authorized to make the request, when it is in line with the will of God and it has the approval of that name on it. As we pray on this earth in Jesus' name, we are speaking in His stead into the situation as a child of the King and the Ascended Lord, using His name with His authority to carry out His will.

This is the very reason why the enemy seeks to downgrade and slander in the minds of men, the name of Jesus. The forces of hell are agitated way beyond our ability to understand, when they hear that name. If the enemy can keep man in darkness concerning the name and can keep Believers from learning to use the name with the authority that they have been given, then he can go forward without hindrance. We, as the warriors of God, are to march forth in the full power and demonstration of the name of Jesus!

The Gifts of the Holy Spirit.

There is much teaching on the Gifts of the Spirit that is available as to the disposition and functioning of these Gifts. Paul said we aren't to be ignorant about them and we are to desire them earnestly. (I Cor. 12:1-13). I believe every Christian should seek to understand the Gifts and how to function and operate in them. They were placed in the Body to help each person and to edify the Body. If ever we needed the Gifts to operate, it is now in this age that we live. They are not natural talents or abilities but they are supernatural in nature. The person does not control them but instead operates under the guidance and direction of the Holy Spirit.

"But the manifestation of the Spirit is given to every man to profit withal. For to one is given by the Spirit the word of wisdom; to another the word of knowledge by the same Spirit; To another faith by the same Spirit; to another the gifts of healing by the same Spirit; To another the working of miracles; to another prophecy; to another discerning of spirits; to another *divers* kinds of tongues; to another the interpretation of tongues: (1 Corinthians 12:7-10)

All of these were given by God to operate in the Body. Every Spirit-filled believer can flow in these gifts. One is not more important than the other, and their operation is by the Holy Spirit. When discussing the army of the Lord and spiritual warfare, there is one Gift of the Spirit that is so important for each believer to wage successful warfare and that is the discerning of spirits.

What is discernment? The definition can simply be put as "the ability to perceive with keenness, insight, and judgment." The word "spirits" here is defined as "pneo" which is "a *current* of air, i.e. *breath* (*blast*) or a *breeze*; by analogy or figurative a *spirit*, i.e. (human) the rational *soul*, (by implication) *vital principle*, mental *disposition*, etc., or (superhuman) an *angel, demon*, or (divine) *God*, Christ's *spirit*, the Holy *Spirit*: - ghost, life, spirit (-ual, -ually), mind."

It is the ability by the Holy Spirit to know whether it is the Spirit of God at work or the spirit of the enemy at work; to know and judge if it is of God. It is not suspicion, criticalness, or being judgmental but instead is clear understanding of knowing the spirit that is behind the situation you face.

In Acts Chapter 16 we see Paul walking through the city when a girl with a spirit of divination began to cry after him saying, "These men are the servants of the most high God, which shew unto us the way of salvation." (Acts 16:17)

Now what this girl said was true, it was not false, but there was something operating through her that was not of God.

"And this did she many days. But Paul, being grieved, turned and said to the spirit, I command thee in the name of

Jesus Christ to come out of her. And he came out the same hour." (Acts 16:18)

What was wrong? A spirit of divination was operating through her and Paul recognized it and cast the evil spirit out.

This is so important for us to understand. In these last days the bible says false prophets, false signs, demonic doctrines and lies would be in the earth. (I Tim. 4: -2, 6: 3-5, II Tim. 3:1-9) Jesus warned of the same thing. (Matt. 24, Mark 13, Luke 21) In order for us to know the counterfeit from the real we must have discernment. What I am about to say I want you to pay close attention to. In these last days strong delusion and demonic lies will be spoken and seemingly accompanied by false signs and wonders. Those without discernment could fall into accepting this as truth.

This should not surprise us for it happened in Scripture when Moses stood before Pharaoh. Moses threw down his rod and it became a snake (a powerful sign and wonder of God) but Pharaohs' men threw down their rods and they became snakes as well (a false sign of the enemy's power as well). However Scripture explains that Moses' snake swallowed those of the magicians. The supernatural is real. The enemy has those who operate in the supernatural realm and can even perform what appears to be "miracles" but when their source is the power of the enemy, it is laced with deception, death and destruction. Scripture warns us to beware of these, who may even appear as wolves in sheep's clothing in order to present a counterfeit of the real and true and all powerful signs and wonders of God.

This should not frighten us or make us immediately shy away from the supernatural realm. God Himself is supernatural and calls us to worship Him in Spirit but also in truth. These things should simply be an alarm to us to walk with sensitivity to the leading of the Holy Spirit. We do not walk in fear but we walk in faith with discernment. The true key is our ability to discern the spirit behind the operation. We need that discernment to know if what we are experiencing and seeing is truly from the Spirit of God. If it is the Spirit of God, one thing is certain; it will always point to and exalt Jesus. Always! If man takes credit for it, it is not of God. A true move of God bears good fruit and it will line up with the whole counsel of God's Word. "Signs and wonders shall follow those that believe." (Mark 16:17&18)

In spiritual warfare discernment is vital to waging the battle and stopping the enemy. Many of our ideas of the spiritual realm have been formed by influence of the world. Viewpoints either ridicule it or over exaggerate it and the enemy uses this so that people will begin to be dull in their thinking and spirit.

Hollywood over dramatizes demonic possessions and portrays demons as being so powerful that good barely overcomes evil. While demonic possession is real and happens today, if we who are in Christ were walking with the power and discernment that God has gifted us with through relationship with His Son Jesus, we would witness lives being set free and demons fleeing as they did when Jesus walked before them.

I once was in attendance at a service where a woman literally writhed like a snake all the way down the center aisle of the church. At other times I have heard voices that were demonic speak through people who were in need of deliverance. I have heard threats and cursing and witnessed people thrown around by an evil spirit. More than all of that, I have been a witness to the demonic spirit leaving when commanded by the authority of the name of Jesus. Confronted with the power of God they had to flee.

Discernment is necessary. We need to pray in this hour that this Gift of the Spirit operates strongly in your life.

Prayer

"Pray at all times (on every occasion, in every season) in the Spirit, with all [manner of] prayer and entreaty. To that end keep alert and watch with strong purpose *and* perseverance, interceding in behalf of all the saints (God's consecrated people)." (Ephesians 6:18 AMP)

Another weapon in our arsenal is the powerful weapon of prayer. Prayer is not a last ditch effort made in a desperate situation. We have all heard the person say, 'Well, I guess all we can do is pray.' It is said as if it were some last remaining thread of hope, however, what it shows is a lack of understanding how vital prayer is.

Warfare is won or lost in prayer. There are things that God has ready for you that will never come into your life unless birthed from the spirit realm by prayer. It is through the avenue of prayer that you enter into the realm of the impossible and make it impossible. Neither is prayer just an exercise of going into God's presence with a list of wants but it is a dialogue between Father and child. It is a communion through which not only do we make our petitions but we also receive from Him direction, strength, wisdom, and instruction. Prayer is a weapon that must be mastered. Everything that we face and everything that we need in order to go forward will come through this time spent in His presence. We must learn the principles that govern prayer. We must understand the difference in the types of prayer. There is the prayer of supplication, petition, agreement, intercession, binding and loosing and the prayer of faith. These must be understood and applied in correct application. Just as in a war there are different calibers of weapons so it is with prayer. The enemy hates us praying and will do anything to try to stop us from praying, including trying to make us think that prayer is futile. There have been many casualties in this war because time was not spent in prayer.

"Confess to one another therefore your faults (your slips, your false steps, your offenses, your sins) and pray [also] for one another, that you may be healed *and* restored [to a spiritual tone of mind and heart]. The earnest (heartfelt, continued) prayer of a righteous man makes tremendous power available [dynamic in its working]." (James 5:16 AMP)

Notice this prayer makes power available to us. Thus, we can understand how no prayer equals loss of power.

"Jesus answered and said unto them, Verily I say unto you, If ye have faith, and doubt not, ye shall not only do this *which is done* to the fig tree, but also if ye shall say unto this mountain, Be thou removed, and be thou cast into the sea; it shall be done. And all things, whatsoever ye shall ask in prayer, believing, ye shall receive." (Matthew 21:21-22)

The mighty, awesome firepower of prayer. Jesus said, "all things." The key to walking in this is abiding in Him and obeying His word. Notice we are to "ask". Some people think the will of God just happens whether we pray or not. They use a shotgun prayer. A shotgun disperses a wide field of shot, hoping it hits something. Many have not learned that prayer concentrated, directed and aimed with purpose, avails much.

Even though God already knows what you have need of, your prayer gives God legal entry into your life and situation. Throughout history God needed men to declare and speak and pray. Jesus instructed us to pray God's will be done. (Matt. 6: 6-13) The principle of prayer is foundational and one we must understand and implement daily.

Prayer takes faith, persistence, patience and action. The enemy fears you praying and seeks to distract you from it at all cost. No teaching, no book, no prayer line, or anything else can ever take the place of having a disciplined prayer life. There is nothing that can replace our time in the presence of God, our ability to enter into His presence and hear Him. He longs with anticipation to speak with us, personally.

The Baptism of the Holy Spirit is essential, not for salvation because you cannot be born again without the Holy Spirit, but for the endowment of power that comes from receiving it. Personally, I do not believe that a person must be baptized in the Holy Spirit to obtain salvation and enter into Heaven. While it is not a salvation issue, the Baptism of the Holy Spirit is for every believer and helps in our fight against the enemy and in living an overcoming life.

Another powerful weapon in our prayer life is praying in tongues or as some say praying in the spirit. Much division arises over this subject and the enemy fights the understanding and the release of it. It is simply a gift given by our Father. When one realizes how powerful this weapon is, it is easy to then understand why the enemy would so want us to be ignorant of its value. On one hand, there has been much taught on the subject in error that has caused people to not even seek it. On the other hand there are those who, being baptized with the Holy Spirit, have not fully grasped the main purpose of tongues. There are some who only focus on one aspect which is the operation of the gift of tongues and the interpretation in an assembly, that they lose sight of the importance of speaking in tongues during their private prayer time.

Through out the years and in various services, I have witnessed the abuses, the disorder and some of the attitudes and confusion over speaking in tongues. It is imperative that we learn to properly move in this gift and speak truth to the misconceptions and confusion over the topic. God is not the author of confusion and He is a God of order. The purpose of speaking in tongues is not to just have an experience or just to operate in an assembly but its main function is in prayer.

Most of the teaching we have on speaking in tongues is from the Apostle Paul. First of all, Paul himself practiced it. Secondly, he said that he desired that all spoke in tongues. Paul clearly gave instruction to the Corinthian church in I

Corinthians Chapters 12 – 14. No where in Scripture can we find where Paul says that tongues are not true, or that they are not necessary. He never states that tongues would end or be done away with, although some have taken the Scripture out of context to build their arguments on the topic. Paul said in Chapter 12 that not all speak in tongues and many have argued this to say that it is only for a select few. However, Paul was instructing them that when gathered in a corporate setting, not everyone is going to move in all the same gifts at the same time. He was explaining order in a meeting and the diversity of the gifts functioning within an assembly.

Paul taught and held the position that all would be filled with the Spirit and that it was available to every believer. Jesus said that it was a gift and He instructed the disciples to tarry for it. They received it and preached it everywhere they went and then Paul who wrote most of the New Testament, testified of it and its function and usefulness.

Praying in the Spirit Helps You to Pray the Perfect Will of God

What we are talking about is a Heavenly language. Do you think it strange that heaven would have its own language? Is it difficult for you to believe that heaven would have its own dialect? If we are able to now embrace the fact that the veil was rent in two and that there is no longer any separation between us and the Father because of the Son, and if we realize that we have the ability to have a conversation with God then we must understand that spiritual truths are spoken in a spiritual language. The natural mind cannot understand it. (See Rom. 8:5-7, I Cor. 2)

"For he that speaketh in an *unknown* tongue speaketh not unto men, but unto God: for no man understandeth *him*; howbeit in the spirit he speaketh mysteries. But he that prophesieth speaketh unto men *to* edification, and exhortation, and comfort." (1 Corinthians 14:2-3)

When praying in the Spirit, it is to God, not to man. It is not to be understood by the natural intellectual, rational human mind. It is your spirit communicating by the Spirit to God. When we pray in the spirit and speak in tongues during our prayer time, it takes away our human side that at times can only think to pray our own will, emotions and needs. The ability to pray in the spirit by the Spirit is a spiritual gift and one that should excite you! Notice too, it says you are praying mysteries.

"So too the [Holy] Spirit comes to our aid *and* bears us up in our weakness; for we do not know what prayer to offer *nor* how to offer it worthily as we ought, but the Spirit Himself goes to meet our supplication *and* pleads in our behalf with unspeakable yearnings *and* groanings too deep for utterance. And He Who searches the hearts of men knows what is in the mind of the [Holy] Spirit [what His intent is], because the Spirit intercedes *and* pleads [before God] in behalf of the saints according to *and* in harmony with God's will." (Romans 8:26-27 AMP)

This is why the enemy hates this and fights it so. He can't understand it! In World War II, when the Marines in the Pacific Theater used bilingual Navajo natives to speak in their native language as a code that was never broken. Not only was the Navajo language used but also others such as Cherokee, Choctaw and Comanche. This was so that the enemy could not decrypt important information as they monitored transmissions. These men were called "wind talkers" and that speaks so powerfully to my spirit of just how the Holy Spirit prays through us.

There will be times when you will not know how to pray for yourself or others. Your own insight and wisdom will not be enough. Yielding to the Holy Spirit and allowing Him to pray through you helps you to pray the perfect will of

God for the situation. It is an awesome thing to know that in prayer you are able to pray in a heavenly code that can not be broken by the enemy and that those very prayers help to bring forth God's perfect will.

Praying in the Spirit Builds You Up

"He that speaketh in an *unknown* tongue edifieth himself; but he that prophesieth edifieth the church." (1 Corinthians 14:4-5)

"But ye, beloved, building up yourselves on your most holy faith, praying in the Holy Ghost." (Jude 1:20)

"But you, beloved, build yourselves up [founded] on your most holy faith [make progress, rise like an edifice higher and higher], praying in the Holy Spirit." (Jude 1:20 AMP)

The word here edifies means to build up and to strengthen! In warfare one gets tired and weary. Many of us have felt worn down from the heat of the battle at times. Praying in the Spirit reenergizes us. This is why it is a necessity to be able to pray in the Holy Spirit. In this hour that we live in we must not grow weary. The enemy seeks to wear us down and drain us so as to render us ineffective. In Daniel Chapter 7 we see one plan of the enemy is to wear down the saints. I believe this spirit is really moving in the land today as we can look around and see so many who are worn down and discouraged. One means of preventing this is to pray in the Spirit. We aren't to grow weary (Gal. 6:9) but to continue fighting with anticipation of victory.

Avail yourself of the power and magnitude of these Scriptures. Through them you shall stand victorious in battle. God has not called you to the battlefield for you to wage this war in your own abilities or strength. He has not left you defenseless before a massive host of the enemy to be a helpless victim. God has provided these weapons to be used by us to walk in overcoming power. Ignorance causes defeat.

We could have the most powerful instruments of war at our fingertips but we have to implement them with accurate knowledge and with purpose. Take them up beloved! Shake off any passivity and grab your weapons and demolish the works of darkness! Ask God to allow revelation knowledge to flow into your life in a new way to better understand the weapons and how to use them.

Chapter 9

Marching Forward

It has been my desire in this book to take you into a study of the subject of the warfare that we are engaged in. The book was designed to guide you in your understanding of the necessity to grasp the reality of the battle and to understand the way to wage it in confidence, faith and determination. God, in His amazing plan, has given us the ability to walk in the victorious life that He has set before us.

The Scripture speaks very plainly on the fact that we will encounter the enemy and that at times we will feel the heat of the battle. God has not left us to our own devices to fight and withstand the enemy, but instead has given us everything we need to walk victorious. We have been called to battle, to wage an affective war on the strongholds and entrenchments of the enemy.

Just as the Civil War was fought for the right of the states to secede and for freedom from the bondage of slavery, we too have been called to bring liberation to men and to help to set the captives free. The Great Commission has called us to bring the truth of freedom to millions who are still in the bonds of slavery to the enemy and to point them to our Lord, Who is the great deliverer. We are to march forward with a liberating word to demonstrate to them that they can walk free from the control and bondage that has held them in chains of darkness. We have been chosen to announce to them that there is freedom available and that they no longer have to be held in the clutches of the despotic ruler who rules this world system. Whatever their chains may be and no matter how long they have been held captive they can walk now free and at liberty. That is the mission of the Body of Christ.

Let there be no confusion concerning the intensity of this warfare. As time goes by the resistance of the enemy will increase. He already knows that judgment has been passed and the soon overthrow of his kingdom will most definitely occur. He continues however to have as many victims as he can capture and destroy as possible. We must remember that every advancement of the Army of God hastens his demise and that he is aware of it. This is why we must begin to fight with fervor as never before. Too long this Army has been silent however it is beginning to awaken with a mighty sound.

I hear the sound of swords rattling and the trumpets of war sounding. God is calling forth His warriors to arise and take the implements of war and push back the darkness and destroy the strongholds. Do you hear that call? Do you sense the urgency in your spirit to stir yourself for battle? Some things are worth fighting for! Arise and fight mighty soldier!

This reminds me of the story in the bible of Shammah. (II Sam. 23). He was one of the mighty men that gathered to David. The Philistines were foraging for food and they came to a lentil patch. Shammah rose up and in the middle of it and fought them and slew them. It tells us that "the Lord wrought a great victory." This was just a bean patch but it was important to Shammah because the enemy was trying to steal it. What is the enemy trying to steal from you? Arise! This warfare will call for tenacity to fiercely fight the enemy with perseverance.

In this same chapter (II Sam. 23) we read of Eleazar who fought with the Philistines until his hand was weary and clung to the sword. Again the Lord delivered a great victory. Are you willing to fight no matter how long it takes to secure the victory? The battle is not always over quickly. In this day and hour everyone wants an instant result but that is not always the case.

"Therefore put on God's complete armor, that you may be able to resist *and* stand your ground on the evil day [of danger], and, having done all [the crisis demands], to stand [firmly in your place]." (Ephesians 6:13 AMP)

Notice it says, "having done all." Whatever that may entail whether it be prayer, intercession, or obeying you must be willing to do whatever the Lord requires you to do. After you have done all that you can do, you are given a command. Stand! It is a military term! In the Greek it means "to abide, continue, and to hold up." It means that we become unyielding to give ground. We do not back off but stay in that place thereby putting pressure on the enemy. This is the place where so many fail because they lack the tenacity and perseverance to hold their ground and continue to resist the enemy. He will always try to get you to retreat, to get your focus off course and to try to get you to look at other things. He wants you to be moved at what you see, to tire you out, or to make you bend in the face of fear.

Faith however enables you to continue to see the victory while refusing to yield to the pressure that the enemy exerts. Stand your ground and refuse to be moved by what you see in the natural. It is always certain that the enemy will start his hardest pressure after you commit to standing, but if you refuse to move, the victory and the breakthrough will happen.

There has been battle after battle in my own personal life that I have seen these principles work when I applied them. There were times that the pressure was incredible and times that I felt like giving in but you see, the victory was important to me. The things that I was standing in faith for were critical to my life.

At the very writing of this book my wife and I have been standing in one particular battle that for us began over four years ago. We entered into a battle that at the time looked totally devastating. The pressure was so intense. The enemy was so trying to destroy our lives and all that we had worked for. Viewing those circumstances with just our natural minds and eyes, it seemed impossible.

When this battle first hit, I knew that I had to begin to rise up and to fight. I did everything that I knew to do. I spent time on the floor on my face in prayer and I walked the floor in prayer. I began to increase my time in the Word of God seeking His direction. It was a hard place and at times I felt such a heaviness and loneliness. I would sometimes just cry and say, "God all that I have is You and Your Word. I throw myself on your mercy and your faithfulness."

At times it seemed as though I was being ignored and my prayers were seemingly (in the natural) not going any higher than my own nose. Every day the pressure seemed to intensify. I did not know how God could turn it around but I trusted His faithfulness. There were times when I would lie down and try to sleep and the taunting voice of the enemy would echo in my mind. To stop this onslaught, I would get up and walk the floor and pray and then praise God in advance for turning it around. Next, I would fall into bed tired and drained.

This went on day after day for several months. In the natural I was doing all that I could do and in the spirit I was doing all I knew to do. Gradually, I began to see God at work in the situation. I continued to see God move in many different ways. I knew He was at work, which would encourage me and so I continued to stand. I knew I had to keep the pressure on the enemy and I knew that the battle was not yet over.

The tendency of most of us is to see a little victory then slack up. It is easy to begin to relax and then forfeit the complete victory. One thing that made me continue pressing in and on is that in the beginning of this the Lord spoke to me and said, "I will restore all the enemy has tried to do to you." I clung to that precious Word with tenacity. From time to time I would just stop and begin to thank God for the restoration He had promised.

My situation didn't change over night and the enemy continued to exert pressure. The circumstances didn't suddenly change in appearance however the circumstances could not move me.

Have you ever felt totally surrounded by the enemy? Everywhere you look it seems he is at work and the forces against you are mounting? I was there! I felt at times like King David, wondering 'How long, oh Lord, will the enemy do this? What else is going to happen?'

I felt like the servant who was with the Prophet Elisha when he looked at the hills and cried out, "We are surrounded, what shall we do?"

We all will have times like that in our lives. Sooner or later we will face a battle where we have absolutely nothing to get us through but God and the truth of His Word. You may feel alone and perhaps feel like your back is against the wall. Realization hits that your wisdom and strength will not be enough. Everything you try seems to make no difference. Like the servant you can only see what your natural eyes can see and you know only that either God brings the deliverance or all is lost.

The Prophet Elisha instructed his servant to fear not. I am sure the servant was wondering, as would most of us, "Is he crazy? Doesn't he see that we are surrounded by the enemy and yet he is saying don't be afraid?" Many times, one can have more confidence in what is seen in the natural than what is promised to them in the reality of the spirit.

At this point Elisha tells his servant that those who are with them are more than those who are with the enemy. Here is where we understand how faith sees beyond the natural. Elisha did not deny the existence of the enemy against them. Faith does not deny the existence of the problem. Instead faith allows us to see the victory in spite of the problem! Faith knows that present circumstances are subject to change.

Elisha then prayed, "Lord open his eyes so he can see." What did he mean? The servant already could clearly see the enemy. Elisha was praying for his servant to see into the spirit realm as he himself was already able to see. Faith always sees into the spirit realm!

The Lord opened the servant's eyes so that he could see that surrounding the enemy as well as himself and Elisha were horses and chariots of fire. The whole time they were there, ready to bring their deliverance. (II Kings 6)

In my own personal battle, as time progressed I saw the Lord begin to move on our behalf. Things began to improve and we began taking back piece by piece what the enemy had stolen. Through out this battle we would rely time after time on the faithfulness of God.

Now four years later, in the middle of writing this book, it seemed that once again the enemy was stirred up, over this same battle that we had stood firmly in God through and witnessed His glorious hand work on our behalf. The enemy came at us once again trying to make us think that he still had our circumstance in his grip. It didn't take long before I began to see into the spiritual realm and I realized that as I have learned victory in Jesus and am about to instruct others in that very topic with this very book, there is an enemy who is furious. Yet, I continued to stand and pray and not give up ground.

As I write this last chapter, sitting next to me on the desk I see a letter that confirms the end of that four year battle and with tears of gratitude and release, I can easily see the greatness of God's love and faithfulness. Here on my desk at the completion of this book, is evidence that God can take the seemingly impossible situations and turn them around. I have evidence that the very principles which I have written about in this very book work for the people of God.

As I look at the letter, I am reminded that the battle at the very beginning looked hopeless and impossible. If you had told us four years ago we would be at this point today, restored by God to the place that He alone has called us to be, honestly, it would have been hard to see it through the smoke of the battle at that time. I know you have been there too.

You have to push through the lies of the enemy being whispered in your ear. You have to arise and declare and boldly believe God. You have to stand in spite of what you see or hear. You have to cling with tenacity to the truth of God's word and fight through every obstacle the enemy puts in your path. At times when you feel like giving up you will find the Holy Spirit empowering you with fresh strength and in those times you will see God moving on your behalf.

As I look back over the whole battle, I see the fingerprints of God's mighty hand upon each detail. What an awesome God we serve!

Remember, battles can make you bitter or better. Adversity has the capacity to overwhelm you, if you allow it to. It is important to keep an attitude of faith and one of maintained peace and joy, no matter what the circumstance looks like. The enemy, who comes to make you give up and turn your back on God, hates it when you are determined to love and praise God anyway.

"The steps of a *good* man are ordered by the LORD: and he delighteth in his way. Though he fall, he shall not be utterly cast down: for the LORD upholdeth *him with* his hand." (Psalms 37:23-24)

Setbacks may come, disappointments at times may arise but we must persevere. We must arise above the taunts and lies of the enemy while guarding our hearts and our minds with all diligence. Your very attitude can hasten your victory or delay your deliverance. We will have the opportunity to give up, grumble, complain, be angry, or whine. We will have the decision to make whether we give in and side with the voice of the enemy or the voice of God.

One of the biggest problems God had in delivering Israel from Egypt was not Pharaoh or his vast army. It did not matter that the Red Sea was before them or that walled cities and giants lay ahead of them. The problem was in Israel! Their attitude is what delayed them the victory. Even in the midst of seeing miracle after miracle and seeing the hand of God move mightily in bringing them deliverance, their attitude grieved the heart of God. It showed a total lack of trust in what God has promised. It showed a lack of thankfulness in their hearts. It cast doubt on God's integrity. What was this attitude that came to the point that it angered God? What caused Him to speak of their attitudes and words as evil?

"Our fathers understood not thy wonders in Egypt; they remembered not the multitude of thy mercies; but provoked *him* at the sea, *even* at the Red sea. Nevertheless he saved them for his name's sake, that he might make his mighty power to be known. He rebuked the Red sea also, and it was dried up: so he led them through the depths, as through the wilderness. And he saved them from the hand of him that hated *them*, and redeemed them from the hand of the enemy. And the waters covered their enemies: there was not one of them left. Then believed they his words; they sang his praise. They soon forgot his works; they waited not for his counsel: But lusted exceedingly in the wilderness, and tempted God in the desert. And he gave them their request; but sent leanness into their soul. They envied Moses also in the camp, *and* Aaron the saint of the LORD. The earth opened and swallowed up Dathan, and covered the company of Abiram. And a fire was kindled in their company; the flame burned up the wicked. They made a calf in Horeb, and worshipped the molten image. Thus they changed their glory into the similitude of an ox that eateth grass. They forgot God their saviour, which had done great things in Egypt; Wondrous works in the land of Ham, *and* terrible things by the Red sea. Therefore he said that he would destroy them, had not Moses his chosen stood before him in the breach, to turn away his wrath, lest he should destroy *them.* Yea, they despised the pleasant land, they believed not his word: But murmured in their tents, *and* hearkened not unto the voice of the LORD. Therefore he lifted up his hand against them, to overthrow them in the wilderness: To overthrow their seed also among the nations, and to scatter them in the lands. They joined themselves also unto Baalpeor, and ate the sacrifices of the dead. Thus they provoked *him* to anger with their inventions: and the plague brake in upon them. Then stood up Phinehas, and executed judgment: and *so* the plague was stayed. And that was counted unto him for righteousness unto all generations for evermore. They angered *him* also at the waters of strife, so that it went ill with Moses for their sakes: Because they provoked his spirit, so that he spake unadvisedly with his lips. They did not destroy the nations, concerning whom the LORD commanded them: But were mingled among the heathen, and learned their works. And they served their idols: which were a snare unto them. Yea, they sacrificed their sons and their daughters unto devils, And shed innocent blood, *even* the blood of their sons and of their daughters, whom they sacrificed unto the idols of Canaan: and the land was polluted with blood. Thus were they defiled with their own works, and went a whoring with their own inventions. Therefore was the wrath of the LORD kindled against his people, insomuch that he abhorred his own inheritance. And he gave them into the hand of the heathen; and they that hated them ruled over them. Their enemies also oppressed them, and they were brought into subjection under their hand. Many times did he deliver them; but they provoked *him* with their counsel, and were brought low for their iniquity. Nevertheless he regarded their affliction, when he heard their cry: And he remembered for them his covenant, and repented according to the multitude of his mercies. He made them also to be pitied of all those that carried them captives. Save us, O LORD our God, and gather us from among the heathen, to give thanks unto thy holy name, *and* to triumph in thy praise. Blessed *be* the LORD God of Israel from everlasting to everlasting: and let all the people say, Amen. Praise ye the LORD." (Psalms 106:7-48)

One thing is certain in the warfare we wage; murmuring, doubt, fear, unbelief, and complaining will be highly displeasing to God.

While my wife and I didn't always have perfect attitudes through out the entire battle that we faced, I can tell you that whenever we would tire or start to give in to the voice of the enemy, the Holy Spirit and the Word of God would rise up inside me. I would feel that corrective nudge in my heart and would repent and arise up in my spirit and fight more. I would correct myself as quickly as possible and as soon as the Holy Spirit began to convict me.

I say this with great love and compassion. When we remain in an attitude of self-pity, grumbling, murmuring, and complaining it doesn't bring deliverance. It will cause a soldier to continue to spiral down in defeat and then in turn cause bitterness. What has happened to you may seem unfair but you have to move forward and rise above it. Put your energy to the battle and not into self-pity. The enemy will do his best to make your attitude opposite of what it needs to be.

If you will arise and march forward with a heart after the King, determined to be pleasing to Him while walking in discipline, endurance, obedience, and faithfulness, ready to follow every command, pay any price exacted, and stand with tenacity and fervor, you will see VICTORY!

"He that overcometh shall inherit all things..." Rev. 21:7

Be blessed mighty warrior and I remind you, as you Arise to the Battle...

"Ye are of God, little children, and have overcome them: because greater is he that is in you, than he that is in the world." (1 John 4:4)

"Now thanks *be* unto God, which always causeth us to triumph in Christ, and maketh manifest the savour of his knowledge by us in every place." (2 Corinthians 2:14)

"For whatsoever is born of God overcometh the world: and this is the victory that overcometh the world, *even* our faith." (1 John 5:4)

"The LORD *is* a man of war: the LORD *is* his name." (Exodus 15:3)

"Lift up your heads, O ye gates; and be ye lift up, ye everlasting doors; and the King of glory shall come in. Who *is* this King of glory? The LORD strong and mighty, the LORD mighty in battle. Lift up your heads, O ye gates; even lift *them* up, ye everlasting doors; and the King of glory shall come in. Who is this King of glory? The LORD of hosts, he *is* the King of glory. Selah." (Psalms 24:7-10)

"For who *is* God, save the LORD? and who *is* a rock, save our God? God *is* my strength *and* power: and he maketh my way perfect. He maketh my feet like hinds' *feet*: and setteth me upon my high places. He teacheth my hands to war; so that a bow of steel is broken by mine arms. Thou hast also given me the shield of thy salvation: and thy gentleness hath made me great. Thou hast enlarged my steps under me; so that my feet did not slip. I have pursued mine enemies, and destroyed them; and turned not again until I had consumed them. And I have consumed them, and wounded them, that they could not arise: yea, they are fallen under my feet. For thou hast girded me with strength to battle: them that rose up against me hast thou subdued under me. Thou hast also given me the necks of mine enemies, that I might destroy them that hate me." (2 Samuel 22:32-41)

"Blessed *be* the LORD my strength, which teacheth my hands to war, *and* my fingers to fight." (Psalms 144:1)

"Fight the good fight of faith, lay hold on eternal life, whereunto thou art also called, and hast professed a good profession before many witnesses." (1Timothy 6:12)

The Warrior!

He was a mighty Warrior and though his hair was gray
The younger warriors listened to all he had to say;
He loved to tell the stories – they loved to hear them too
As he described the battles the boys' excitement grew.

The shields of the young warriors was wonderful to see
They knew that they were ready to face the enemy;
And as the battle started – their victory seemed sure
But as the pressure mounted their strength could not endure.

The older Warrior listened as the younger warriors cried
We did just like you told us but we very nearly died;
We challenged all the powers - we thought that we were strong
We memorized your strategy but where did we go wrong?

The Warrior drew them close to him and spoke out of his heart
I told you of the battles but that's not the place to start;
It's not a flair for glory - that keeps a sharpened sword
But a warrior is a lover who's devoted to his Lord.

You see I just took for granted that you already knew
The source of your endurance does not spring forth from you;
Oh but you must keep rekindling – the flame of bridal love
The battle may be here on earth but the victory is from above.

This was a painful lesson but I think you learned it well
You love the Lord of Heaven and then you fight the prince of hell;
Now if you will remember - these words I say to you
Maybe you'll live long enough to be old Warriors too.

Words by Clay Mclean
Clay Mclean Publishing Co.
Copyrighted

About the Author Dennis O'Daniel

Revivalist and Teacher Dennis O'Daniel and his wife Vicki reside in Ohio.

Dennis has evangelized through out the United States and overseas with a burning purpose to teach the uncompromised Word of God, under the anointing of the Holy Spirit, with a desire to reach the needs of the people through the Gifts of the Spirit.

Through his ministry, the yoke of bondage has literally been destroyed off the lives of many as the Holy Spirit prompts, directs and leads him during times of ministry. With a purpose and vision to fully equip the body of Christ, he has personally developed extensive training materials and has taught these in segments which include series topics such as The Fire of God, The Holy Spirit, The Fruit of the Spirit, Gifts of the Spirit, Confession, Fact or Fiction, Take the Higher Ground. Also a singer and songwriter, he ministers through music and has recently recorded a Gospel CD, "I'll Sing My Song" with songs of faith; three of which he wrote. Dennis is a graduate of Faith Bible College in Tyler, Texas. In 1978, after graduation, he was ordained as a minister and traveled around the country and to Africa spreading the Word of God.

Dennis O'Daniel Ministries

"Impacting the World with an Impacting Word"

To Contact the Ministry:
Dennis O'Daniel Ministries
P.O. Box 537
Monroe, Ohio 45050

On the Internet:
www.dennisodanielministries.com

LaVergne, TN USA
08 April 2011
223438LV00001B/17/P